The

SELF

Improved

The
SELF
Improved

*The Scientific Way
To Get What You Want*

Donald Spector

>)) hatherleigh

www.hatherleighpress.com

Visit www.TheSelfImproved.com for more information on *The SELF, Improved*, workshops, assessments, and the author.

Library of Congress Cataloging-in-Publication Data is available.
ISBN 978-1-57826-335-6

The SELF, Improved is available for bulk purchase, special promotions, and premiums. For information on reselling and special purchase opportunities, call 1-800-528-2550 and ask for the Special Sales Manager.

10 9 8 7 6 5 4 3 2 1

Printed in the United States

Disclaimer
For educational purposes only, this book offers suggestions and recommendations for healthy eating and exercise. The suggestions and recommendations in this book are not to be considered as any form of medical advice, direction, diagnosis or treatment and are not intended as a substitute for the advice of a licensed healthcare professional. The reader should consult his or her doctor before commencing any diet or exercise program based on the contents of this book.

"Don Spector's incredible insight comes from his understanding of how things in our world fit together, how to improve them, and then capturing the ideas that capture the imagination. His application of this skill set to the human condition makes for an exciting personal opportunity for each of us who reads this book."

   —**The Hon. Michael Balboni,** *former New York*
      State Senator, former "Homeland Security Czar"
      for New York State

"Don Spector's lifestyle has been very impressive and supportive for me. His spirit is to enjoy everything; the best time of his life is always now."

   —**Jitsuro Terashima,** *Executive Managing Officer;*
      President, Mitsui Global Strategic Studies Institute,
      Mitsui & Company

"Don Spector's *The SELF, Improved* will be an inspiration to any student of self-improvement and personal growth. Don Spector was (and still is) a friend and mentor to me in the '90s, during a personal career low. His guidance and tutelage helped me not only reinvent myself and get me back on course, but showed me that there is a better and easier way to get where I need to go. *The SELF, Improved* will do for you what it has already done for me. . . attain greater success and reach loftier heights."

   —**Dee Snider,** *radio and television personality, actor, writer,*
      producer, announcer and lead singer of Twisted Sister

"My teaching is similar to the molecular model. I look at the big picture and take one small step at a time to help each individual reach their goal."

—**Nick Bollettieri,** *founder of the Nick Bollettieri Tennis Academy, legendary coach to ten #1 tennis players in the world including Andre Agassi; Boris Becker; Martina Hingis; and Venus and Serena Williams*

"Buddy Hackett called Don a dreamer, who within his dreams has visions. He brings those visions to life daily. He has integrity and patience. He guides people in the direction they are heading; always allowing them to make the call. It was a privilege for Buddy to be a friend of Don's. I feel this book will impart tremendous knowledge to those who are looking for guidance."

—**Sherry Hackett,** *widow of Buddy Hackett, the legendary comedian and actor*

"Don Spector recognizes the best in everyone, even in a child like I was when I met him. He helped me believe in myself, taught me how to cultivate my strengths, encouraged me to pursue what made me happy and how to reach my goals. I am forever grateful for the opportunities he has given me. While everyone does not have the chance to be personally mentored by Don, this book, *The SELF, Improved,* is the next best thing. The book captures his personality and the lessons in life that he taught me over the years which I still use every day."

—**Mary Rodas,** *youngest member admitted to the Hispanic American Hall of Fame*

"If I lived in the year 1910, I would have been friends with Albert Einstein. I, as an artist, had the honor of painting an Albert Einstein portrait for the Einstein estate. Don Spector is the Einstein of today. Don is creative and just simply a genius. But also Einstein wasn't a business person, Don is. Don has his right and left brain going. I am sure this book will become a bible to many."

— **Steve Kaufman,** *internationally acclaimed pop artist and former assistant to Andy Warhol*

"Our friendship means a great deal to me. Your work ethics and your beliefs have helped so many people. I know this book will change many lives."

— **Jerry Vale**, *renowned recording artist*

Dedication

This book is dedicated to my wife, my immediate and extended family, my friends, business partners, associates and the companies that allowed my ideas to come to fruition.

It is also in memory of my brother, who died too young to realize his potential.

Contents

A Note to the Reader

Wherever you are in life right now, and no matter what you want to do, be or obtain, this book will help make it possible. *The SELF, Improved* is based on a patented process known as the Science of Self-Improvement, an analytic way to make big changes happen by breaking them down into smaller "molecular level" changes.

In fact, the original title for this book was *The Molecular Model for Success*. The "molecular model" for success approaches the changes you want to make in life by breaking them into many, achievable small steps. Through a system of honest assessments of your strengths and weaknesses, as well as your goals, you will discover that the sum of these changes results in larger accomplishments than what seemed possible. You will feel more confident and others will see you differently. This is the key to attaining your goals.

The skills that you will acquire through reading and utilizing the assessments and charts in *The SELF, Improved* can be applied in numerous ways to attain any of your life's objectives. . . whether in the workplace or in your personal life.

If your path or goals should change over time, the techniques you will have learned from reading this book will still guide you. The tools in *The SELF, Improved* will become your most valuable asset.

No matter what your goals may be, *The SELF, Improved* is your key to making your dreams a reality.

Introduction

Everything we do, everything we read, everything we see and every experience we have, influences how we live. We are the product of genetics, environment and experience. Our ideas and the way we look at the world have been taught to us by our families, friends and our local communities. We are influenced by the media, what we select to read, what we are required to read, and of course, our teachers, our leaders and the underlying philosophy of our country. We are also influenced by our religions and traditions.

Our culture can even determine how we see ourselves. Concepts of beauty change from one part of the globe to another, and even from one generation to another. In some societies, being overweight is regarded as a sign of wealth; in other societies being overweight is viewed with disdain. Had we been born in another part of the world, we would probably conform to the standards of beauty there, as well as their standards concerning religion, education and culture.

In the United States, the Declaration of Independence states that "all men are created equal." Although this document ensures that we are equal under the eyes of the law, most of us know that when it comes to our social standing, physical appearance and other factors, we are all far from being treated equally.

1

As Plato wrote in *The Republic*, ". . . Democracy . . . is a charming form of government, full of variety and disorder, and dispensing a sort of equality to equals and unequals alike."

We are not all the same, and we are not all equal in our abilities. A person who is 5 feet 5 inches tall knows that the odds are against him if he wants to be the center for a professional basketball team. Of course, this doesn't mean the person cannot attain wealth and privilege and have many other opportunities. What we should remember from this example is that we have to look at what we have, what we want, and then, through careful scientific analysis, determine what we can achieve. That is the subject of *The SELF, Improved*.

Many people don't like change. They are in relationships they don't like, or live in a place or have a job they don't like, simply because they are too lazy to change. Many people put more time into evaluating a financial investment than they do into evaluating the investment they make in the only life they have. When people are in these relationships, jobs, cities or countries they don't like, they tend not to perform at their best, and therefore compound the problem by never attaining what they could have had otherwise.

Everything that we have learned and all of our life experiences can have value for the future. Even if we change our professions or careers, we should never look back at the past as a waste of time. The value of certain occurrences may not be immediately apparent, but all experiences and all learning can change our perspective and make us unique. This new, unique perspective affects us and directs us as we go forward in the direction of our goals. It is important to understand that experiences from our past can be of value even if those events are far behind us. We need to understand this; otherwise we will inadvertently make the job of changing that much more difficult.

It's difficult to change professions, careers, and relationships. But it is never too late.

Grandma Moses, who painted her first painting at the age of 76, is an inspiration to all who think that it is too late to make a change.

Life is too important to waste on something that you do not enjoy.

In order to benefit most from the Science of Self-Improvement you must be totally honest about the way you look at yourself. This book has a series of assessments. The assessments are a mirror, designed to show you who you are and help you decide what you want to do. Then—most importantly—this book will show you how to achieve your goals.

Cheating is simply cheating yourself, because if you don't see yourself the way you are, others will never see you the way you want them to see you.

The Not-So-Magic Mirror

In the fairy tale Snow White, *the magic mirror that told the Queen that she was the fairest maid in the land did not change the way other people saw her. In fact, if the Queen had had access to the self-improvement tools, cosmetic enhancements and surgeries we have today, she could have looked as beautiful as she wanted—if she had really "seen the truth" about herself.*

People have many more opportunities than they did in the past to be who they want to be, as long as they don't delude themselves into believing that they are happy when they are not, or deceive themselves into being someone they are not.

You can change your life if you let yourself. The knowledge presented in this book will help you do so.

Clearly, a book is not going to turn an ugly man into Brad Pitt. However, a book can change your life if you let it.

Self-improvement may be difficult or it can be easy. It depends how much change you really want in your life and how much you want to improve. It's no different than changing the way you look: you can use makeup, or, in extreme cases, you can avail yourself of plastic surgery. One is easy; the other is more expensive, but has more dramatic results.

There are no certain answers that I, as the author, can recommend. Instead, there are questions that I will ask. *It is up to you, the reader, to answer these questions to determine how much improvement you really want.*

In his book *Alice's Adventures in Wonderland*, author and mathematician Lewis Carroll describes a sequence in which Alice asks the Cheshire Cat, "Would you tell me, please, which way I ought to walk from here?" The Cat responds, "That depends a good deal on where you want to get to," to which Alice replies, "I don't much care where—." The Cat then asserts, "Then it doesn't matter which way you walk."

If you really don't care where you are going in life or business, then it really doesn't matter much which door you take. If that were the case, you wouldn't be reading this book.

The SELF, Improved is designed to help you succeed in the workplace, in your personal life, and in your community. Of course, all of these—your job, your relationships, and your life—are intertwined.

The first assessments will enable you to discover how happy you are with yourself the way you are now and how much improvement you really want ... and where you really want to go. While there is always room for improvement, to some it will be much more important than others. If you can't get the job you want, or you're not in the career that you want, or on the right path that you want, this book will require a lot of work.

If you are basically happy with where you are in life and just want to improve your odds of greater success, this book may seem easy for you. However, the more important you are in your present position, the greater your rewards will be from even the simplest of improvements. For example, when I advise influential people in government or business, individuals who have obviously already achieved a great deal of success, the application of the principles in this book can be of even more value to them, since they can easily incorporate them into their own world. The difference between winning and losing is often a fine edge. Like a trained athlete in a championship game, the difference between victory and defeat can often come down to a minor adjustment.

Some things are easier to change than others. Poor speech requires a lot of work to overcome. On the other hand, changing your hair color is very easy. Either one of these may have an effect on your life, depending on what you do. This book allows you not only to take a look at yourself and your abilities, but also helps you establish priorities so you can attain your objectives.

Behavioral Objective Defined

A behavioral objective is something you seek to accomplish in the context of an interaction. You should walk into a situation with a behavioral objective in mind and, hopefully, walk out knowing your behavioral objective has been achieved.

Keep your outcomes in mind. Behavioral objectives are extremely important in order to help you decide which things to work on and where you want to go. Many people go through life without having behavioral objectives. This is a mistake I see people make over and over again.

Every time you go into a meeting, every time you are in a relationship, you should know what you want to take with you when you leave.

Here's an example: A salesman goes into a meeting to get an order. There is a famous line that says, "Once you get your order, leave." It's amazing how many salesmen keep talking after they get their order. Continuing to talk after you've obtained your behavioral objective, of course, has no upside. The only thing you can possibly achieve by further talk is to unwittingly lose the order! In a meeting, when you get what you want, leave. In social relationships things are more complicated, but the principle remains the same: if a relationship is working, go with it; but, just as in finances, *don't put good money after bad and don't waste more time after you've wasted time.*

Don't get too hung up on the numbers in the assessments. They are only there to make it easier to have a quantitative way of looking at things in your life that are really qualitative. If they become an annoyance, just breeze through them, do them quickly and use them as a guidepost rather than as a textbook.

Prioritizing skills is what you will do when you rate your attributes. Whereas a lot of people do this from a subjective point of view, doing it with numbers and putting it down on a piece of paper is the easiest way to achieve your goals in this area. You achieve your goals by seeing what is most important to you and by seeing how you perceive your own qualities. This will allow you to set your priorities for what you want to achieve. Whether this is in negotiation, an image or an impression, a job interview, a paper, or a report, it is the same system. The numbers will help you turn qualitative information into quantitative information that you can use in your everyday life.

But like everything else, you get out of it what you put into it.

FIRST
SELF-ASSESSMENTS

Before you begin reading *The SELF, Improved*, take the time to honestly evaluate where you are in life at this current moment. In the next few pages, you are invited to assess your perception of yourself. By reviewing, rating and comparing your personal attributes to your values, you will identify the areas that you will want to prioritize and strengthen as you read through this book.

You may not fully understand the meaning of each attribute at this point. That is okay. Make your best judgment according to what you believe these attributes mean. As you read the book, you will gain a clearer understanding of each of these attributes. Later, you will be able to re-assess your strengths once you have gained greater knowledge and insight into their meanings.

These charts were created to help you establish your priorities. Be honest and direct with yourself. Use them as a mirror reflecting the "true" you. These are the areas you believe to be important to you.

Keep in mind that, if you change your mind about your priorities as you read the book, you can revise and make changes as needed. It is most important that you be honest with yourself, so you should not hesitate to revise those priorities if, the first time around, you wrote something down that you thought you wanted but that really isn't what you want. The basic rule is that you can fool other people, but don't ever fool yourself; it is a waste of everyone's time.

CHART I:
PERSONAL ASSESSMENT

On a scale of 1 to 10, in your opinion, how do you rate yourself on these traits?

Go down the entire list and put a number after each attribute. (1 = not good at all and 10 = the very best.)

You can give the same rating to more than one trait.

Your honest opinion of yourself	
ATTRIBUTES/TRAITS	Rate each item on a scale of 1-10
Overall Appearance	9
Dress Well/Nice Clothing	10
Healthy Weight	9
Hair	10
Grooming	10
Facial Appearance—Skin/Makeup	10
Overall Physical Carriage	9
Posture	9
Body Language	9
Open/Confident/Poised	9
Strong/Vibrant/Energetic	9
Overall Communication Skills	9
Speech	9
Writing	9
Good Listener	10
Clarity	9
Speaking in Public	9
Overall Intelligence and Aptitude	9
Educated	9
Experienced	9
Street Smart	9
Talented	9
Well-Versed in Current Affairs	9
Good with Numbers and Math	9
Read and Write Well	7
Overall Personality	9
Confident	9
Ambitious/Motivated	9
Serious/Reliable	9
Friendly/Happy	9
Caring/Considerate/Tolerant	9
Patient	8
Relate Well to Others	9
Cool Under Pressure or Stress	8
Overall Professional Skills	8
Leadership	9
Organized	9
Multi-Tasker/Time Management	8
Preparedness	9
Motivator	8
Computer Ability	5
Clear Thinker	9
Overall Etiquette	9
Personal Manners	9
Business Manners	7
Overall Health	10
Physically Fit	10
Eat Well	9
Sleep Well	10
Strong/Vibrant/Energetic	10

CHART II:
IMPORTANCE RATINGS

On a scale of 1 to 10, in your opinion only, how important are these traits to you?

Don't consider other people's values— only your own. What attributes do you admire most and wish for in your own life?

(1 = not at all important and 10 = the most important.)

Rate them all. You can give the same rating to more than one trait.

How important are these traits to you?	
ATTRIBUTES/TRAITS	**Rate each item on a scale of 1-10**
Overall Appearance	
Dress Well/Nice Clothing	
Healthy Weight	
Hair	
Grooming	
Facial Appearance—Skin/Makeup	
Overall Physical Carriage	
Posture	
Body Language	
Open/Confident/Poised	
Strong/Vibrant/Energetic	
Overall Communication Skills	
Speech	
Writing	
Good Listener	
Clarity	
Speaking in Public	
Overall Intelligence and Aptitude	
Educated	
Experienced	
Street Smart	
Talented	
Well-Versed in Current Affairs	
Good with Numbers and Math	
Read and Write Well	
Overall Personality	
Confident	
Ambitious/Motivated	
Serious/Reliable	
Friendly/Happy	
Caring/Considerate/Tolerant	
Patient	
Relate Well to Others	
Cool Under Pressure or Stress	
Overall Professional Skills	
Leadership	
Organized	
Multi-Tasker/Time Management	
Preparedness	
Motivator	
Computer Ability	
Clear Thinker	
Overall Etiquette	
Personal Manners	
Business Manners	
Overall Health	
Physically Fit	
Eat Well	
Sleep Well	
Strong/Vibrant/Energetic	

CHART III:
ATTRIBUTE PRIORITIES

Do you currently possess the attributes you admire and think are important? Do you have them at the level you believe you should? The good news is that you can improve!

To identify your goals and priorities, subtract your Importance Rating (Column B) from your Personal Rating (Column A).

Any Negative (-) number indicates the need for some work on your part. The lower the number, the more you need to focus on this attribute.

These will become your goals and priorities. Copy your answers from Charts I and II to calculate your priorities.

For Example

Let's say you're examining how well you dress. First, you weigh your own ability to dress well. After honest consideration, you rate yourself a 7 (in Column A). Then, because you value this attribute a great deal, you give it a rating of 10 (in Column B). Notice, because you rated this trait's importance as 10, when you subtract Column B from Column A to obtain the result in Column C, you get a negative number (7-10 = -3).

Attributes with negative numbers in Column C are the ones you will seek to improve. They are your goals and priorities.

A larger negative number means there is a strong disparity between your current perception of yourself on this trait and the importance of this trait to you. You will need to put more effort into this attribute to attain your own goal in this area.

You may also want to review the lower positive numbers (A − B = 0 to +2). While there may be no need for improvement according to this result, you should always maintain an open mind and strive to improve these and all attributes.

ATTRIBUTES/TRAITS	A. YOUR HONEST OPINION OF YOURSELF (copy from previous Chart I)	B. HOW IMPORTANT ARE THESE TRAITS TO YOU? (copy from previous Chart II)	A – B = C (+ or -) Negative #'s are your Priorities
Overall Appearance			
Dress Well/Nice Clothing			
Healthy Weight			
Hair			
Grooming			
Facial Appearance—Skin/Makeup			
Overall Physical Carriage			
Posture			
Body Language			
Open/Confident/Poised			
Strong/Vibrant/Energetic			
Overall Communication Skills			
Speech			
Writing			
Good Listener			
Clarity			
Speaking in Public			
Overall Intelligence and Aptitude			
Educated			
Experienced			
Street Smart			
Talented			
Well-Versed in Current Affairs			
Good with Numbers and Math			
Read and Write Well			
Overall Personality			
Confident			
Ambitious/Motivated			
Serious/Reliable			
Friendly/Happy			
Caring/Considerate/Tolerant			
Patient			
Relate Well to Others			
Cool Under Pressure or Stress			
Overall Professional Skills			
Leadership			
Organized			
Multi-Tasker/Time Management			
Preparedness			
Motivator			
Computer Ability			
Clear Thinker			
Overall Etiquette			
Personal Manners			
Business Manners			
Overall Health			
Physically Fit			
Eat Well			
Sleep Well			
Strong/Vibrant/Energetic			

1

Your
FIRST IMPRESSION,
Improved
Manage the Impression You Make

"It is quite possible for people who have never met us and who have spent only twenty minutes thinking about us to come to a better understanding of who we are than people who have known us for years."
—MALCOLM GLADWELL
Journalist and Author
Blink: The Power of Thinking Without Thinking

In his book *Blink: The Power of Thinking Without Thinking,* author Malcolm Gladwell describes how decisions are often made on first impressions—in the blink of an eye. The first encounter is very important when meeting prospective employers and in personal and professional relationships.

We all want to make a certain impression. We all have images of ourselves. Conveying the image of ourselves as we want others to see us takes time and work. How to do that is the substance of this chapter.

There are many elements that together form an impression that others have of us. Sometimes a person can have one overwhelming trait that characterizes them. For example, a 7-foot 2-inch person will often be confused with a basketball player no matter what he does for a living.

Beautiful actresses in Hollywood are often thought of as stupid because of the stereotype depicted by early Hollywood movies. Marilyn Monroe was a highly intelligent woman, but the public often saw her as a dumb blonde because of her appearance. Yet, whether an impression is true or false is irrelevant. Each person has to decide for himself what impression he wants to give to other people.

Unfortunately, people like to stereotype. Therefore, the impression that you give should try, as much as possible, to fit into people's preconceived stereotypes. This may go against your instincts to be seen as an individual; but whether you like it or not, first impressions are stereotypes. Your clothing, your grooming and your physical appearance are all going to be stereotyped. If you are overweight, it is going to convey a whole set of characteristics about you that may or may not be true. Conversely, if you are in good shape physically, people have a different impression of you. If you speak well people will think that you are educated.

Cutting It Close

In the early '70s, when I had extremely long hair, I got a short haircut so I looked conservative and could carry out my assignment with important Mexican officials. I knew that in Mexico long hair was discriminated against by the government law enforcement officials, so I did what I needed to do to best accomplish my behavioral objective.

Judging a Book by Its Cover

My Fair Lady *is a play based upon the assumption that if a girl from the streets could be taught to speak well, society would mistake her for royalty. In the original play,* Pygmalion, *George Bernard Shaw took one component of a person's social impression and made it the key of society's overall impression of her. Of course, in the play, he also changed her basic appearance and seemed to disregard the impression that her appearance made, concentrating on her vocal skills. A fact of life is that people often form impressions based on a package. That package, then, forms the stereotype.*

It is against the law to discriminate against people for all kinds of reasons. However, without saying so, many people—including prospective employers—exclude people based on first impressions. First impressions really are a form of discrimination. On the other hand, discrimination is a fact of life.

Generalizations, while sometimes superficial, can also be extremely important. In jungle training, for example, survivalists learn that snakes with triangular heads are often poisonous. This is a generalization. On the one hand, it can save a life. On the other hand, it threatens the integrity of non-poisonous snakes that happen to have triangular heads. Generalizations tell us that if a piece of metal is red hot it will burn us. They tell us that if milk smells bad we should not drink it.

Oftentimes, social norms trump scientific laws or rules of nature. When this happens, people try to pretend otherwise and cover it up. But it still happens. Be aware of how people stereotype, discriminate against, and make generalizations about others. Once you understand this, then you can go with the flow.

As they say on Wall Street, the trend is your friend.

IDENTIFY YOUR IMAGE

Where do we begin this process of projecting an image that we want other people to see us as? It starts with the most dominant impression that we want to leave with people.

Do you want people to see you as attractive? Do you want people to see you as intelligent? Do you want them to see you as physically desirable? Or do you want them to see you as very competent? Obviously, most of us want all of the above. Obviously, most of us can't get all of the above. Here is where the selection process takes place.

This is a good time for you to look back at your initial assessments, where you established your priorities, and see what it is that you consider most important. It is also a time to change those priorities if, deep down, you wrote something that you thought you should write down but it isn't really what you want.

It might seem superficial to write down that you would prefer to be seen as attractive rather than perceived as intelligent. But don't rate "intelligent" over "attractive" if that's not what you really want. Be honest with yourself.

This book emphasizes that which is most important personally to you. If you put down something that is inaccurate, you will end up following the wrong path.

Go back and look at your priorities again and make sure they are in line with what is in both your heart and your mind.

GET "SOMETHING FOR NOTHING"

Everybody should try to improve all aspects of themselves, to the extent that it is possible. Regardless of your objectives, it is always a good idea to try to "get something for nothing." Getting something for nothing is relatively easy to do when it comes to making a first impression. This is why every lawyer tells the defendant to walk into court wearing a suit and tie, a pantsuit or skirt and jacket. Why? Because it shows respect for the court. Courtrooms are formal places. Going into a courtroom in jeans and a black leather jacket creates a bad impression on the judge and jury no matter what you were accused of doing. While the defendant is certainly not going to be acquitted of a crime because he is well dressed, it will help his case.

This same principle can be applied to a job interview, getting a new account, making sales calls, or even social activities. When going to a job interview, you want to fit in with the corporate culture of that environment. This is one reason why, before going to the interview, it is a good idea to go by the place, see what other people are wearing, see how other people on the job are behaving—for example, if they are more casual or more formal in their behavior—so you can better "fit in" on your job interview.

KNOW WHEN TO COMPROMISE

"Fitting in" doesn't mean that you should try to become a clone of everyone else. What it does mean is that you may have to compromise and adjust your image if it is important enough to you to achieve the behavioral objective of working for that company. Most of the people hired by a company fit a profile that the management and human resources department prefer in an employee. If you can happily live with that profile, then take the job.

If, however, you really don't think that you fit in at all, or that adhering to their standards will be too much of a compromise for you, maybe you should skip that job and move on to a company that will be a better match for you. Life is difficult enough without trying to conform to being somewhere you don't belong. "Fake it 'til you make it," is an expression used in Alcoholics Anonymous. This approach may work at low levels of a company or in casual personal relationships, but at higher levels of a career or in more intimate relationships, "faking it" seldom works. Of course, "faking it" doesn't generally apply to pretending to like wearing a tie. That is, most people will accept that compromise and, if an employer wants them to wear a tie, they will do it. Don't be stubborn and refuse to wear one—and then lose your career because of it.

Some organizations carry their rules to ridiculous extremes.

Extreme Exclusions

Jimmy Carter was not allowed in the dining room at the Plaza Hotel while wearing one of his famous sweaters because a jacket was required of all guests. Clearly the President of the United States was not going to bring down the image of the Edwardian Room at the Plaza. However, many people function as automatons, and you can be specifically excluded from things that you really want for silly reasons.

Nonetheless, as silly as an employer's rules may seem at first, if the job is important to you, take the time, make all the compromises you can, and do your best to get the job. Again, this does not mean that you should compromise your convictions for money or a job—that's another way of "faking it," and it won't work anyway. Compromise is the name of the game when it comes to the impression that you make, but for all of us, *there are things that cannot be compromised.*

Take the time to know when compromise is required, and carefully gauge what compromises you are willing to make.

STRENGTHS AND WEAKNESSES

Everyone has strengths and weaknesses. You want to emphasize your strengths.

Covering up your weaknesses, however, does not mean being deceptive. You'll only end up hurting yourself in the end. You're not going to succeed at a job that relies on strengths you don't have and exposes weaknesses you've covered up.

Although you should never be misleading, there is no reason you should call attention to your weaknesses. Place weaknesses firmly in the background, put your best foot forward—and, on your own time, work to improve, as much as possible, those areas that are weaker than others. When presenting yourself to others, you can use your strengths to guard your weaknesses. Ultimately, you can survive at a job that requires you to use your strengths and, with a minimal level of work, also hide your weaknesses.

With your first impression, you want to look intelligent, pleasant, and healthy. You want to behave in a way that is energetic and conveys that you are someone with whom it is easy to get along. You should be well dressed, consistent with the dress code of the organization, and be as well spoken as possible. You must strive to develop each of these traits according to your priorities, and maximize your point of diminishing returns. In this context, "diminishing returns" means that the less you have to do to achieve your goal, the better. If you're going to a job interview or heading off to a day at work, odds are you don't need to look like a movie star! Do enough, but there is no need to overdo it.

If you can get yourself to a point that you look good—maybe even better than those around you—*you can stop there.* Don't spend too much time trying to be the most glamorous person in the world. If you do, you risk not only creating jealousies around you, but you also risk neglecting some of the other basics that you need in order to be well-rounded.

MAKING A FIRST IMPRESSION
FOR THE SECOND TIME

You have probably heard the expression, "You only get one chance to make a first impression." It's an old saying but it's not always true.

Hollywood is full of movies in which a man who has only seen a woman with her hair pulled back sees the same woman with her hair down for the first time, and all of a sudden he views her in a whole new light. In fact, you could say that he *really* sees her for the very first time. . . even though he has, of course, seen her many times before.

While Hollywood may exaggerate reality, it does reflect the truth to some extent. If you get past the first barrier and become a part of the corporation, personal relationship, or social network, there is room for you to change other people's first impressions of you. This principle is about interpersonal relationships, both personal and professional. Obviously this works both ways. A boss can change his or her first impression of you, whether you intended it to happen or not . . . otherwise, people wouldn't be fired, nor would they be promoted. Dismissals and promotions are based on both the progress somebody makes on the job, as well as mistakes that the human resources department has made in initial hirings.

LIVE UP TO YOUR FIRST IMPRESSION

While the first impression is important to getting you in the door, you really don't want to waste your own time, or the time of the people on the other side of the door, if you're not going to be able to really live up to that first impression.

Lying is a mistake that a lot of people make when looking for jobs. People falsify their resumes, lie about their experiences, and pretty much do whatever it takes to get a job. More often than not this can lead to disaster in both your personal life and your professional career. Aside from being wrong, it leaves you with a sword over your head. Lying on a resume is grounds for immediate dismissal, should the employer ever find out. If the job is not going to be a win-win situation for the employer and the employee, then don't waste their time—or yours. Life is too short. Furthermore, by lying your way into one job, you're depriving yourself of another opportunity that might come from somewhere else.

Improve yourself by following the basic rules, but don't try to become someone that you're not or don't want to be. It won't work. *Again, don't fake it 'til you make it.*

SELF-ASSESSMENT QUESTIONS

- Do you know the kind of first impression you want to make?
- Have you identified which areas are most important to you?
- Do you know the impression you actually make?
- Have you identified where you would be willing to compromise?

2

Your
IMAGE,
Improved
Improving Your Physical Self

"Always be a first-rate version of yourself, instead of
a second-rate version of somebody else."
—JUDY GARLAND
World Famous Vocalist and Actress

Focusing on your self-image and learning to improve it is important for many reasons. A good self-image is not just of use when you are looking for a new job. It is also vital when you are looking to advance in your current job or in your personal relationships. Being successful in any and all aspects of your life requires that you focus on your self-image.

Self-image is composed of many different elements, some physical, and others more abstract. All require attention, awareness and conscious effort.

THE PHYSICAL ATTRIBUTES
OF SELF-IMAGE

Dress the part. How you dress is one of the easiest things to change and is one of the most important in creating an impression. Again, a good part of what we are going to be talking about is what image you want to convey to others, and a big part of your outward image is how you dress.

While dress can express individuality, it is also, in many cases, reflective of a culture and specific to an organization or association. Before any meeting, learn as much as you can about the people attending and where you will be meeting, to make certain you are dressed properly for the event. If you are uncertain, it is always acceptable to ask in advance what attire would be considered appropriate.

Choose your colors. Color is an important element of a person's image. The right color clothing for a person can enhance their features and give them an extra edge. Popular culture even says that "blondes have more fun." This may or may not be true.

Experts can advise you on what colors look best on you and what is most flattering for you. Incorporating the right colors into your wardrobe is an easy, inexpensive shortcut to enhancing your image. Also, avoiding the wrong colors can be just as important.

Your personal grooming habits. For men and women, personal grooming includes hairstyle and physical appearance and, for women, the use of cosmetics. Personal grooming, combined with dress, round out the elements that make up the "Blink" effect and, if used properly, can ensure that you communicate the image you want.

Advice from Experts

ELEMENTS OF GOOD GROOMING

Be clean. Shower and bathe regularly. Be sure your hair, nails and clothes are always clean.

Smell clean. Use deodorant or antiperspirant and don't overdo cologne or perfume.

Maintain good oral hygiene. Throughout the day, make sure your breath is fresh. Use a breath spray or mints to prevent bad breath.

Wardrobe. Make sure your clothes are stain-free, well-pressed and fit you well. Fit is more important than the cost or quality of your clothes. A crisp, professional suit can look shabby with scuffed shoes. Check yourself in a full-length mirror before you leave the house.

Shave (for men). Men should either be clean-shaven or have well-trimmed facial hair.

Hair care. Consult an expert who can help you determine the best cut for you, given your hair texture and shape of your face. Then, maintain that style with regular trims.

Cosmetics (for women). You can learn about makeup for free at any department store cosmetics counter. Pay attention to the way the salesperson applies makeup so that it is most flattering for your features and skin type. You can also pick up makeup tips in most magazines.

When to Consider Plastic Surgery
by Richard Karpinski, MD
Harvard Medical School Graduate, Board Certified Plastic Surgeon, Board Certified General Surgeon

Using Plastic Surgery techniques as a means to "Your Self Image, Improved" is perhaps a drastic approach compared to many of the other strategies enumerated in this book. Nonetheless, Plastic Surgery (and in this term I will include all kinds of techniques: filler injections, Botox treatments, dermabrasions, chemical peels, and laser treatments as well as the more invasive operations with incisions and sutures) deserves at least a small consideration in this publication. So it is appropriate to ask, "Can Plastic Surgery be used as an appropriate approach to self-image improvement?"

Although some Plastic Surgery is motivated by vanity and is intended more as a personal improvement than as a way to connect better to others, there are almost always subtle (or not so subtle) effects in the interpersonal arena; Plastic Surgery can provide a definitive boost to interpersonal impressions.

The lead-in to this chapter is a brief excerpt from Malcolm Gladwell's book *Blink*. One of Gladwell's core ideas is that we are programmed to make some decisions about people based on nearly-instant impressions. Among the factors subconsciously included in such lightning assessments are, unavoidably, physical appearance, body language and carriage, and tone of voice. And I would argue that Plastic Surgery can have an effect on all of these cues.

Just as the songbird with more brilliant plumage or more symmetrical patterns attracts a potential mate's attention as being fitter, or stronger, or more successful, we are attracted by people with "prettier" or more balanced features. As one patient of mine—a talented artist—put it, "You won't get anywhere without the talent; but, without the best appearance, the conversation that divulges your talent never happens; attractiveness is the foot in the door for artistry in the real world—especially for women."

To take things one step further, improved appearance frequently does make a positive change in self-esteem, and this is often reflected in carriage, grooming, and how one speaks. So a successful Plastic Surgery intervention may affect your "Blink" moments by changing the way you behave. Two dramatic examples from my own practice are the nine-year-old girl who lost her speech impediment once her "Dumbo" ears were corrected, and the thirty-five year-old teacher, who became much more poised and effective with his students after a rhinoplasty reduced what he saw as a "gigantic" nose.

In the performing arts, there may be a strong and direct need to maintain a nearly ideal physical appearance—whether by makeup, Botox, clever clothes/hair styling or cosmetic surgery. Although there are counter examples (Joaquin Phoenix, Stacy Keach: cleft lips; Forest Whitaker: wandering eye), there is enormous pressure from agents, photographers, producers and the tabloid press for stars to look flawless. For most of us, thankfully, the push is not so great.

While some lines of work value maturity, seriousness, and experience, others put a premium on youth and good looks. In these competitive workplace environments—especially those dominated by young people (for example, advertising, sales, software, finance, public relations)—one's appearance by surgical rejuvenation techniques (from filler injections to facelifts to liposuction) may help a patient to secure a job or retain one in the face of younger challengers. Many middle-aged men will seek facelift surgery before they hit the job market, feeling this move is as important as brushing up their resume.

Even in less competitive work environments, or in the circle of friends and family, patients often seek Plastic Surgery to address a familial facial feature that is misconstrued by the people around them. These misapprehensions may drive patients to frustration or cause them to feel excluded from some social events. Patients will often come to a consultation complaining that "everybody keeps telling me I look tired—even if I've had a good night's sleep," or reporting that "my family tells me I am sour because I look like I'm frowning all the time," or "I'm really not overweight, but the stuff hanging under my chin makes everybody think I'm fat." Once the frown lines, or double-chin, or baggy eyes are fixed, the patient often reports a dramatic change in attitude from their co-workers, friends, and family members—even though the patient is spiritually/emotionally unchanged.

My inference from these situations is that Plastic Surgery does have a place in the multitude of ways to improve your self-image. Plastic Surgery affects the way you look and feel, and therefore, how you project yourself with friends, family, employers and spouses.

THE LESS TANGIBLE
COMPONENTS OF SELF-IMAGE

Your manner of speech. There are two components of speech: the first is *what* you say; that is, content. The second is *how* you say it, which is pronunciation. Both are equally important.

Content is easier to address than pronunciation because, to improve content, you can read, study and research to discover meaningful, relevant information. Pronunciation, on the other hand, may require professional attention, particularly if English is not your first language or if you have a heavy regional accent. In cases like these, you may need the help of a professional speech coach. *Although accents can be an asset, you want to make sure that what you are saying is clear and understood at all times.* If an accent interferes with understanding the content, it can become a source of conscious or unconscious discrimination.

Attitude is key. Impressions are not just about looks, clothing, speech, fitness and poise. They are also about the attitude that you convey to others.

You want to project a positive image of who you are. That might be an image of power, an image of caring, or an image of professionalism. These images are communicated and picked up by others through your body language and your personal style.

Sometimes, conveying power can be accomplished with minimal verbal communication. In *5 Steps to Professional Presence: How to Project Confidence, Competence, and Credibility at Work*, authors Susan Bixler and Lisa Scherrer Dugan describe a technique called "soft power." To practice this technique during a meeting, start by keeping your contributions to a minimum.

Instead, focus intently on the person who is speaking. Then, when everyone has had a chance to weigh in, sum up the best of what was said and add your own perspective.

As Bixler and Dugan state, "Nonverbal communication validates all our verbal information, and it is always more believed than anything we say."

You can act assertively and try to show others your ideas, or you can act passively and try to show others how attentive you are. The important thing to be aware of is that these traits can be taken positively or negatively depending on the situation.

For example, a person of power may be perceived as pushy in a social situation, whereas, in the office, the same person can be seen as a great top-level executive and a leader. The difference can depend on the culture you are in at the moment. If you are a very assertive person and you are dealing with people from a less assertive culture, you should tone down the volume of your voice and even the color of your tie. *For example, don't wear a bright red tie to a meeting with Japanese executives. Power ties can come off as threatening.*

If, however, an organization is looking for someone to run the department, you might want to show that you're also willing to work many hours, take control, and be assertive. *So the situation helps to define the behavior.*

Learn listening. Become an active listener. Many people don't listen to what other people have to say. Not only does this put them at a disadvantage, but it offends the other person. It is always best to understand the other person's point of view. Even if you are dealing with an adversary, you want to know how he thinks; you want to know his vantage point. It is similar in a military situation: when possible, you want to *know how your enemy thinks in order to defeat him.*

You always lose an opportunity when you don't know what the other person is thinking. The easiest way to do this is to listen to and try to understand him.

Advice from Experts

EMPLOY THE TECHNIQUE OF ACTIVE LISTENING

Although it would seem to be largely intuitive, active listening, or simply listening to others, is a skill that requires certain guidelines. While reading the following, consider the fact that active listening is, at its most basic level, an extension of the Golden Rule: listen to others as you would have them listen to you.

Minimize external distractions. Close your reading materials and turn off PDA's, cell phones, televisions and computer screens.

Face the person addressing you. Show you are paying attention by using body language: sit up straight or lean forward slightly depending upon your comfort level.

Maintain eye contact without staring or defocusing.

Minimize internal distractions. Disregard your internal thoughts and continuously refocus on the speaker. Don't think about your upcoming response. Let the speaker finish and then let the conversation flow naturally from there. If necessary, jot down quick notes or a word that will remind you later of what you want to respond to.

Keep an open mind. Let the speaker finish before you jump to conclusions.

Respond and show you understand. To keep the conversation moving in its natural rhythm, only interject with short phrases such as, "uh-huh," "really?" or "interesting!" Use body language like nodding at the right time to show you grasp the speaker's implications.

Don't Interject. Avoid interrupting to give advice by sharing a similar experience of yours and don't jump to defend yourself, even if the speaker is launching a complaint against you. This way, both sides will have the whole story and you'll be able to address the entire issue at once.

Engage yourself. When the speaker has finished, feel free to ask questions for clarification. This way, you haven't interrupted their train of thought and you can take the time to repeat the most important points back to them.

CONVERSATION SKILLS

Learn to be a good conversationalist. Strive to join in the conversation at hand. That does not mean that every time somebody says something you have to try to "one up" them. Rather, try your best to participate in discussions with other people.

However, this doesn't mean that you have to participate in a discussion that you don't understand. If you don't understand what people are talking about, say something. Even saying, "I don't understand," is better than just sitting there without comprehending.

Participating in a discussion can be as simple as asking a question.

Interaction is the key to being a good conversationalist. Engage the other person and bring out the best in them, too.

Advice from Experts

3 WAYS TO IMPROVE CONVERSATION SKILLS

Be genuinely interested. Genuine interest in another person and the topic at hand is essential to keeping the conversation going.

Try to make the other person feel comfortable. Smile and appear friendly. This will make the other person feel comfortable and help them open up to you.

Give the other person time to think and respond. Don't talk so much that the other person doesn't have time to respond.

A Great Host

Johnny Carson was one of the best talk show hosts in the history of television. It wasn't because of his personal talent; it was because he brought out the best in other people. This wasn't the case for all celebrities, but networks often forgot this: it was always surprising to network executives that some of the biggest comedians could not carry a talk show. This was largely because the comedians kept trying to be the act themselves, as opposed to bringing out the best in their guests. This was what prevented them from having enduring careers such as Johnny Carson's.

BODY LANGUAGE

Body language is an extremely important part of the image that you create. Body language is defined as the gestures, movements, posture, alertness and mannerisms by which a person communicates with others. It can make you look threatening; it can make you look vulnerable; or it can make you look self-confident. It is an important part of how people see you.

If you look too tough, people are not going to feel relaxed. Consequently, they won't open up to you. Having people open up to you is extremely important. When people feel comfortable around you, it allows you to obtain your objectives.

Body language also tells people who to go to for answers, in everyday life as well as emergencies. It is part of what constitutes leadership. Body language can inform people that you like them or you are in charge; it's also a way of showing that you're not interested, and can make or break your relationships, depending on the situation.

Advice from Experts

THE BASICS OF GOOD
BODY LANGUAGE

No matter what you may be saying, your body can give you away—body language is considered to be the subliminal expression of emotions and state of mind.

Posture. Slouching and leaning to one side tend to indicate disinterest and apathy. For this reason, make a conscious effort to straighten your back when standing and to lean in slightly when sitting.

Handshakes. When shaking hands, the most important thing is making palm-to-palm contact. After that, try to match the amount of squeeze given to you.

Eye contact. Eye contact is another thing that requires practice and an understanding of your own comfort level. In some cultures, extended eye contact is considered a confrontation and an attempt at domination, while in America it usually indicates honesty and good character.

Arm and leg position. When standing, keep arms loose and open. Folded arms across the chest can indicate confrontation, defensiveness or boredom. Feet should be no wider than shoulder-width apart. When seated, always sit tall and avoid moving your legs.

Body Language Can Decide an Election

George Bush Sr. made a basic mistake during the 1992 Presidential TV debate with Bill Clinton by looking at his watch. The public interpreted this action to mean that he wasn't interested in an important debate. Many thought that this was partly responsible for his defeat against Clinton. Clinton, on the other hand, was a master at body language. He always communicated interest in the speaker and focused on that person completely to ensure conversations were productive. Ultimately, he used body language to win over even his enemies.

In most people's lives, each of these factors will play a minor role, but the difference between success and failure is often a fine line. This book can give you that extra edge in life. Combined, these self-image tools can give you the advantages that you need to gain greater self-confidence, to get you the jobs that you want, to get you into the social settings and the personal relationships that you want and to make you more productive in all your endeavors. Depending on which attributes are most important to you, based on your priorities, you can use these skills in your everyday or professional life.

SELF-ASSESSMENT QUESTIONS

- What can you immediately do to improve your self-image and how people see you?
- Are you a good listener? Do you really hear what people mean?
- Are you a good conversationalist?
- Does your body language reflect well on your presentation of your self-image?

3

Your
MEETING SKILLS,
Improved
The Doorway to Your Future

"Never wear a backward baseball cap to an interview unless applying for the job of umpire."

—DAN ZEVIN
Humorist, Essayist and Author

Job interviews are "meetings" with prospective employers. So, many of the skills explained in this chapter can be applied not only on job interviews but also when meeting with your boss, another department in your company, or with an outside client.

In reading this book, a number of topics will overlap and some of the information is redundant. This is because many of the same tools that are used in personal life can be used in your professional life. However, it is better to be redundant than to forget those tools that you need to obtain what you want in life.

Job interviews are a way for you to get into a system that can help you launch or advance your professional career. The object of a job interview is not to fool the potential employer. Rather, the goal is to find a job that is a good fit for you. Keep remembering, this is your life. If you take a job that is not right for you, and fool the company into hiring you, not only are you wasting your time, you are keeping yourself from true success opportunities.

People who advance in their careers tend to be good at what they do and enjoy the work they do.

IT'S A TWO-WAY PROCESS

All meetings, including job interviews, are a two-way process. Think of it that way and it will make things a lot easier. In fact, your potential employer probably experiences a similar type of anxiety as you do. As Richard Nelson Bolles and Mark Emery Bolles advise in *What Color is Your Parachute?*,

> As you go in to the interview, keep in mind that the person-who-has-the-power-to-hire-you is sweating too. Why? . . . [Because]...any or all of the following:

- ...you won't be able to do the job: that you lack the necessary skills or experience, and the hiring-interview didn't uncover this.
- ...it will take you too long to master the job, and thus it will be too long before you're profitable to that organization.
- ...you will do only the minimum that you can get away with, rather than the maximum that they hired you for.

DO YOUR HOMEWORK

The company is looking at you and you are looking at their organization. However, you shouldn't wait until the moment of the interview to find out about them.

Before you go into a job interview, learn about the company. Find out what they make or market, who their customers are, what their mission is, and what their objectives are. You want to read up as much as you can about who they are and how they do things.

The Truth Behind a Company's Future

When you are looking for a job and are considering joining a large company, you may think that because they are a large organization, they are doing well. However, today the truth is that you never know how well a company is doing—and you never really know why they are hiring. Unfortunately, some companies hire people because they know that they will have to lay people off later and they want new people to lay off. Obviously, stay away from those companies.

COMPANIES IN TROUBLE
AND FAMILY BUSINESSES

However, companies in trouble sometimes present an opportunity. It's a little bit like trying to advance in the armed forces during wartime. While war is hell, it also presents a better opportunity for current soldiers as well as new recruits to advance more quickly than if they joined in peacetime. The same is true for companies in crisis. It gives certain types of people with abilities the opportunity to show their talents, which might not have surfaced otherwise. People can rise very quickly if they have new ideas that can help a company in trouble, and when the company is back on its feet *these people will be part of a turnaround team.*

It is also important to look at the management and the ownership of the company. Family companies can be a dead end. At the end of a long, hard career, too many people have found out that the key positions go to family members. Blood is thicker than water, and while a lot of people may think they are the exception, family companies tend to promote family members.

Advice from Experts

FIVE WAYS TO LEARN MORE ABOUT A COMPANY

Review their web site

Read their literature

Try their products

Pay attention to news about their business

Discover their values through advertising, leadership, and promotional materials

---

THE NEXT STEPS

After you have checked out the company and determined that you like their products, their mission, and what they stand for, what is the next step? You've found them to be reasonably stable and you think you might have an opportunity at that company. Now, how do you get the job?

You start by organizing those things that you can "bring to the party." Think of your own skills and knowledge base and how what you possess might be of value to that particular company. Include these things in a cover letter and also in your resume. Use the following tips, and remember: *never lie in your cover letter or resume.*

Advice from Experts

KEYS TO SUCCESSFUL RESUME WRITING

Remember to consult your charts where you identified what you want and your prioritizing of the different attributes.

Have an objective before you start writing. Know what you plan on doing and your resume will be far more cohesive. You do not want an unfocused and unorganized resume.

Think of your resume as an advertisement. Your resume is a pamphlet promoting a great new product sure to revolutionize the industry: YOU. You're selling yourself, your skills, abilities and your talents. You want to be clear and concise so you can get an interview. During the interview, you can explain, in depth, the importance of each point you've made.

Start with your strengths. Your resume will only take about 30 seconds to get scanned from top to bottom by most human resources representatives; make sure the most important skills for your objective are listed first.

Make it easy to read. Bullet your sentences and start them with verbs. Resumes are generally scanned and a bulleted sentence format allows the reader to quickly gain a thorough understanding of your skills. Use clear headings and occasional bold type. Add words like "organized, outsold, improved, engineered, increased or delivered" throughout. These "action" words highlight your accomplishments and bring you and your resume to life. Numbers (#), dollars ($) and percentages (%) all stand out in a resume. They show that your productivity was measured not only with action verbs, but with proven results.

Know the field. If your particular field uses specific terminology, don't forget to place those words in your resume.

Get your resume reviewed. You may understand what you mean, but it's not always clear to everyone else. Have someone else point out exactly what they don't understand so you can fill in gaps and correct mistakes.

Send out your resume. Apply for jobs below, at and above your level of experience and secure as many interviews as possible. At the interview, you may be surprised to learn that the jobs above your level could actually be easy for you. No matter what happens, it is better to send resumes for jobs at all three levels and have some poor interviews than to send resumes only on your level and hear nothing back.

Advice from Experts

KEYS TO SUCCESSFUL, EFFECTIVE COVER LETTER ETIQUETTE

Be brief. A cover letter should be only one page long and should include a statement of intent, with the resume and any supporting materials attached.

Revise, revise, revise. A single error—in grammar, the company name, address, or spelling—and your cover letter will not be read. Reread it before you send it.

Keep it simple. Use business fonts like Arial or Times New Roman in black and white only, with 10 or 12 point type.

Keep it neat. Your cover letter should be well-organized and should have the addressee, date and proper greeting on the top. The body of the letter should come next, followed by your signature.

COME PREPARED

Make sure you bring with you to the interview, or any meeting, everything that you need. Remember, the more you bring, the more likely it is that you can close the deal. That is what you want to do: close the deal, get the job, get the order or whatever your behavioral objective is, and not leave it open-ended.

To do this, you must provide all the materials that they need to check you out. So before you go to the interview, prepare copies of your resume, copies of your references—and anything else that you think you may need to verify to the company that you are telling them the truth about who you are. Remember, just like you checked *them* out, they have to check *you* out too. So make it easy for them. They will appreciate it, and you will also hasten the process and increase your chances of getting the job.

HOW TO PRESENT YOURSELF

There is a great line in Rod Stewart's song, "You're in My Heart," that says, "Her ad lib lines were well rehearsed." In the job search world, and in many other business and personal situations, I think this suggests that while you are trying to give the impression of spontaneity, you also want to think out very carefully how you want to present yourself and how you want others to see you.

This idea was discussed earlier when you rated those traits that you think are most important in defining yourself. This is where you're going to emphasize those points that are the strongest and try to minimize your weaker points. Just as you never lie in a resume or cover letter, you should never lie in a job interview, or in a meeting or interaction. As I said, *this is your life, and if the job, situation, or relationship is not right for you, you don't want it. So forget about whether or not you can get it.* Remember how hard it is to change; don't get into something you don't want in the first place.

STRATEGIES FOR
SUCCESSFUL INTERACTIONS

During any encounter with people who can help you obtain your behavioral objective, whether you are going into a job interview, sales call, or meeting, relax and think of the person or people you are engaging with as potential friends. Of course, we don't tend to interview or try to sell something to our friends, but we also don't get nervous around them or worry about losing them (if we did, they wouldn't be our friends!). So be calm, be professional, use the tools that you learned in the previous chapters, and think of your potential employer, customer or business partner as a friend. In fact, if things end up working out for you both, that is what they will become.

Remember, take note of what the people you are meeting or interviewing with are wearing, know their way of thinking, and try to blend in, while at the same time try to show that extra spark that you alone can bring to the situation. When questions come up that you find difficult, take your time. You can ask them to rephrase the question in a different way. But don't cover up anything you've done in your life. This is the same as you would do in friendships—*if people cannot accept you for who you are and what you've done, they're not really your friends. Forget them and move on to an environment where you will be appreciated.*

Be honest. No matter what questions you are asked, be honest. In an interview, you may be asked about your schooling. If you were not a good student in school, just say so. But also, find a way of answering that frames things in a positive light by adding statements about other accomplishments or attributes. Remember the example of the salesman who keeps on talking after he has gotten his order—there is no reason for him to go on and on if he has sealed the deal. If things are going well, remember your behavioral objectives and don't speak for the sake of speaking. While you have to be honest when answering questions, certainly never volunteer anything that could put you in a bad light.

Maintain eye contact. Keep looking at the speaker and make eye contact. This is important in almost every social interaction, including job interviews, sales calls, and meetings. People like to see other people's eyes—they think you are telling the truth when you can look them straight in the eye. Try to make this as much a two-way interaction as is possible.

Maintain energy and focus. Remember to look alert, even if the person you're meeting with seems a little bit disinterested. After all, you're trying to get the job, close the sale, achieve your objective, or otherwise persuade your audience.

For an interview, keep the following in mind. It makes a difference if you are interviewing with a human resources (HR) person or the person with whom you'll be working. If you are interviewing with the person with whom you'll be working and that person does not respond to you, it may be a very troublesome sign at this early stage. However, if you just need to get past the interview with an HR person, just think of it as if you're required to wear a nice jacket to get into a fancy restaurant. The important thing is not your wardrobe; it's getting past the entrance so you can sit down and enjoy your meal. That is, do whatever is necessary to advance beyond the HR interview. Listen, act alert, and try to get to the next level: an interview with your potential boss.

Rehearse. Some people recommend role-playing and working with a friend or colleague to practice for job interviews, meetings, or other business transactions. You can do this either formally or informally. It might be a better idea to try to put together the image that you want to convey and try out that image and your "ad lib" lines, as opposed to rehearsing for a specific job interview or meeting. If you are conveying the image that you want to convey and the people you are interviewing or meeting with don't like it, chances are good you don't want that job or that client. Always listen to what others have to say and remember that you can learn something from everyone.

Anticipate Common Questions

During an interview, if you are asked questions such as: "Can you stay late? Will you be here in emergencies? How much of a priority is your job to you?" you, of course, want to respond that your job is very important to you, but it wouldn't hurt to engage in a discussion, too.

You can ask what kinds of opportunities are available for those people who throw everything into the company. Broaching this topic doesn't mean that you will immediately ask, "Will I have comp time?" or "Do I get extra pay for that?" Those kinds of responses show a lower level, short-term way of thinking in a potential employee.

Instead, you want to ask, "Can people who make this company a priority in their lives move up in the company?" This is a perfectly legitimate question and the answer can provide you with valuable information.

Have a positive mindset. Sometimes we hear rumors that certain people are hard to get to or hard to work with. Forget the rumors—assume everybody is your friend. Be friendly and professional. Believe that you will be able to handle the situation. This doesn't mean that you should let your guard down or tell secrets or make yourself vulnerable. What it means is don't ever go into a job interview or any meeting with a negative attitude.

Find common ground with your interviewer or potential client. You may be surprised: you may have grown up in the same state, gone to the same school, or you may know somebody in common. Any of these things will give you a big advantage in the interview.

Finding Common Ground. . .
A Key to Successful Negotiating

I was negotiating a dispute with one of the largest companies in the world, with lawyers entrenched on both sides. I fired my lawyers and decided to take over the case myself. It happened to be the holiday season and I made sure that I ended all correspondence by saying, "Best wishes for the holiday season." After a couple exchanges, I started getting back responses that also wished me the best for the holiday season. I knew then that I would make a settlement, which I did soon after.

Little things are important. Little things can make a difference between getting what you want in life and losing everything. Try to find a common ground with people. There is always a common ground. Sometimes you have to look deeper but it's always there.

Hostage negotiators have to go into the worst situations with some of the worst people in the world. They try to make contact with them and find some common ground. It's not always easy, but they know other people's lives depend on it. You may not be in that kind of situation but you can use the same tools. . . even in a job interview!

Speak with integrity. The worst thing that can happen in a job interview or meeting is if they catch you in a lie. That pretty much terminates everything. *Don't do it.*

Lying is especially bad in a job interview. If you have something in your past and it comes up, just admit it and *move on!* If the interviewer can't get past that, then forget the job. This is just like in personal relationships. If something went wrong in your earlier life that the person you're meeting cannot accept, you don't want to continue the relationship. Keep remembering that this is not a one-way street. You only have one life and you don't want to waste your time in a career or in personal relationships with people who are going to hold something against you for the rest of your life. That's their problem. There are plenty of other people who will accept you for who you are.

Aside from everything else, lying to a potential employer deprives you of all your rights in the company thereafter. That is a big deal. It means that all the time you invest after you get the job could be wasted if, for any reason, they wanted to get rid of you. *Don't do it.* Have more self-respect and know that somewhere there is the right job for you.

Demonstrate follow-through. Just as in sports, follow-through is an important part of every game. Every golf or tennis player knows that hitting the right shots doesn't mean that he's won the match. Every stroke has to be followed through properly to give it that extra strength. No win can ever be assumed before the game is over. This is especially true in job interviews: make sure that you follow up with whatever you promised to give them, as well as a *letter* thanking them for their time and interest in you. The letter should be appreciative and genuine, and it should also include details about your meeting to remind the interviewer who you are, and demonstrate that you were engaged and focused during the interview. Follow-through is very important.

A thank you note is also an effective tool to use after a meeting or business encounter. As Richard Nelson Bolles and Mark Emery Bolles state in *What Color is Your Parachute?*, "A thank you note jogs their memory." It helps the interviewer or business associate remember who you are, and helps them recall what you told them you would do for them.

Advice from Experts

HOW TO WRITE A
THANK YOU LETTER

Write your letter immediately. Shortly after the interview, meeting, or work event, write your thank you note(s). If you don't, it can reflect poorly on you or simply allow the people who you met to forget you.

Write different notes for each individual that you met. Separate notes illustrate that you see the interviewers, associates, or potential clients as individuals and that you possess writing skills.

Keep it positive. Make your note short but be sure it isn't formulaic, boring, or poorly formatted. Be positive and do your best to assure the person reading it that, if they hire you to work with them, you will bring benefits to the workplace.

SELF-ASSESSMENT QUESTIONS

- Do you highlight your strengths in all situations?
- Have you thought through what skills you can bring to the job, relationship, or situation?
- Do you keep your objective in mind when interacting with other people? Do you usually obtain that objective?

4

Your
SPEAKING SKILLS,
Improved
How to Communicate Effectively

"The difference between the *almost right* word and the *right* word is really a large matter—'tis the difference between the lightning-bug and the lightning."

—Mark Twain
Great American Author, Essayist and Humorist

This chapter identifies the basic elements of effective speech. It will assist you in learning how to express yourself with greater ease, accuracy and clarity. As you learn these skills, you will gain confidence in speaking and develop fluency, conviction and effectiveness for all your interactions, professional and personal.

CONTENT IS KING

While there are many rules that you will learn and shortcuts that can be of help to you, there is nothing more important than having something to say. Express it in the best way possible.

If you don't know what you're talking about, as P.T. Barnum, the great showman and circus master, said: "You can fool some of the people all of the time, and all of the people some of the time, but you cannot fool all of the people all of the time."

So the rules you are about to learn assume the basic premise that *you have something to say that is of importance and of interest to the people to whom you are speaking.* Otherwise it doesn't really matter how strong your vocabulary and grammar skills are, or your use of nonverbal communication, or how good your pronunciation is, or how well-chosen your visual aids are. Unless you have something of importance to say, all the tools that enable you to speak better and with confidence will be useless.

THE IMPORTANCE OF CONTENT

Though it might seem like a given, what you have to say always has to be more important than your presentation or delivery. In some circles, the presentations themselves can actually seem more important than the content, but this effect is generally short-lived.

A Great Presentation. . .
A Poor Ad Campaign

I was working with a fragrance company where an ad agency was making a presentation to the top executives on a new commercial. They devoted three hours to describing the nuances of this 30-second TV spot. They spoke beautifully, using perfect grammar and sophisticated vocabulary. They were confident, and spoke with ease and clarity. They were well-organized and their visual aids were great. The entire presentation focused directly on their objective. In other words, they utilized many of the keys to success you will learn about in this chapter. They obtained their behavioral objective and secured their client. The advertisement was bought by senior management of the company and the TV commercial was produced and aired extensively.

Unfortunately, although the agency obtained their objective, they didn't achieve their goal, because the TV viewers didn't have three hours worth of explanation of what the commercial meant. Instead, they only had that 30-second ad. The television spot was not able to convey to the public what the ad agency had communicated to senior management during the meeting. Therefore, the product failed, and the ad agency was eventually fired.

This example illustrates two points: one is that there are short-term and long-term behavioral objectives. Everything was good about the ad agency's presentation, and they secured their short-term objective. However, their long-term objective failed.

The second point is that this story is a tribute to the power of a good presentation. It is also an important example that you should remember for long-term success: your presentations are a tool to strengthen other people's ability to view and understand your product or recommendations. You must make sure that the content of what you are presenting is accurate and truthful.

PRECISION VS. ACCURACY

In physics they teach you the difference between precision and accuracy. Somebody can take a ruler and very precisely measure that something is 3.152 inches. That is precision. But if the ruler is incorrect, however precise the number is, the result is not going to be accurate.

Accuracy is the truth. *Precision* is the detail into which you go when measuring something.

Precision is a lot like the tools you use for making a presentation or speaking to someone. If you use the tools in this chapter properly, they will enhance your presentation and general communication. However, there is no substitute for accuracy of content. Great tools cannot make your message truer if the content is not accurate.

All I am going to do in this chapter is teach you how to present something in a better way. *It is up to you to make sure that the content is worthy of the presentation, conversation, or discussion.*

FIND WHAT MAKES YOU
MOST COMFORTABLE

"According to most studies, people's number one fear is public speaking. Number two is death. Death is number two. Does that sound right? This means to the average person, if you go to a funeral, you're better off in the casket than doing the eulogy."

—JERRY SEINFELD
Television Personality and Comedian

A lot of people have trouble speaking in front of groups and being the center of attention. The trick here is having *self-confidence* and *self-esteem*. For some, speaking to groups creates pressure. People have different ways of coping with being under pressure.

My own personal formula, in any competition or in any setting, is to start out in my mind with the premise that I've already lost, and therefore I have nothing left to lose. This puts me at rest. It allows me to joke around, to be self-assertive, to be myself and to pretty much do whatever I want, knowing that I can only better my position, since in my head, I started with the premise that I had already lost. A lot of people will tell you that this is the complete opposite of the self-assertive premise of going in and thinking that you're a winner.

This is my way, and all this tells you is, "To each his own."

Everyone can find something that makes them feel comfortable. Whatever is in your head that makes you relax, learn it and use it. Many professionals imagine their audience naked as they sit in their seats. If you have trouble relaxing, you might want to speak to a friend, a business associate, a family member, a psychologist or somebody else who knows you, and who can help you find what works best for you. This is because the ability to feel at ease and comfortable when you're speaking to others is one of the most important tools that you can use to become an effective communicator.

PREPARATION IS THE KEY

One of the most important things in making a presentation and to help you be relaxed is to be prepared. In fact, if you were to do the research, you would find that preparation is the key to some of the most effective presentations.

Preparation will help you feel confident. You can usually have more confidence when you have had a rehearsal, when you've already gotten some feedback from others, and you're not treading new ground for the first time. Furthermore, preparing in advance allows you time to carefully choose your words and catchphrases, and identify other elements that will help you during your presentation.

Advice from Experts
_____

HOW TO CREATE
AN EFFECTIVE PRESENTATION

Have an agenda. Stay aligned with your agenda while you prepare. Don't just think about your objectives; think about the objectives of the recipient of the presentation.

Know your audience. Every effective communicator knows to whom he's speaking. Assess the knowledge of your listener. Is this person more or less knowledgeable than you? Is he or she an expert? Are they knowledgeable about other subjects but on par with you, prior to your research?

People are often offended when someone attempts to tell them something that they already know; without even knowing it you could insult the very person you are seeking to enroll in achieving your goals. Research all the authorities in the subject material, making very sure not to include rudimentary subject material that could offend the other person.

Adjust the tone. The tone of your message also has to be in proportion to the subject you are dealing with. Is this subject personal? Does the subject have a universally emotional impact? Is the subject impersonal, intellectual or controversial? The answers to these questions will determine the appropriate tone of your delivery. A newscaster reporting on the death of people who have been killed in a serious accident would lose his job if he were jovial. Serious material calls for a serious tone. Also keep in mind, though, that a good professional presentation featuring impersonal material can be enhanced by humor, anecdotes or interesting bits of information, as appropriate.

Be clear. Clarity is essential in order to deliver your message and achieve your objective. Some people think that if they use complex language that speaks above the knowledge of the audience, it will make them look intelligent. Quite the opposite is true. Make your material simple to understand. If you believe it will be difficult for the listener to grasp, use examples from everyday life such as metaphors or analogies, visual data, personal examples, or materials gathered from science, media or the marketplace.

If you are not clear, you will have a much more difficult time engaging the person or audience in your objective or goal.

Use visual aids. Only use visual aids if they will enhance your presentation; otherwise, you risk overwhelming your audience. Utilize color, shapes and pictures. Vary fonts and type sizes and add relevant photographs or examples.

Be positive. *Never be negative.* You will alienate your audience. Especially in today's marketplace where so much about the future is uncertain, being positive is a great asset. Never make other people look bad. Instead, find a positive way to deliver any news, no matter how negative.

Keep on track. Keeping on track is an important part of organizing your presentation. Whether your presentation is oral or written, use the same skills to create an organized template with which to make your case. I suggest PowerPoint® as a way of helping you organize your thoughts so that they can be presented in a logical way. PowerPoint however, should only be used to communicate something of real importance, not just a simple concept.

Remember, people tend to go off track when they don't have an outline for their presentation. It's pretty difficult to go off track when you're scripted.

Make eye contact. When speaking to a group, keep making eye contact with one or two persons to make sure that you don't lose the people in the audience. They provide you with feedback, and, by looking at your audience, you know, at any given moment, how you are being received. Talk directly to them. If you lose them, find something you may have in common with one of them to bring them back, like asking your audience "Does anyone have any questions?" Your audience will appreciate you speaking directly to build a rapport.

If your presentation is verbal only, be sure to move your body and establish a comfortable rhythm in order to hold the attention of your audience.

THE ROLE OF
NONVERBAL COMMUNICATION

There is a big difference between verbal and nonverbal communication. In this chapter you are next going to explore the role of nonverbal communication.

A Hero. . . with a
High Pitched Voice

In the early days of Hollywood, during the era of silent movies, there was nothing but nonverbal communication. Stars used their bodies and faces to express the feelings, challenges and crises of their characters. The best became big because of their ability to tell the story through nonverbal communication. As a matter of fact, many of these stars were unable to make the transition to talking pictures because their verbal skills did not match their nonverbal skills. No one expected a Western movie hero to have a high pitched voice!

Imagine that you are required to give your presentation without words. Practice giving your speech in front of the mirror without speaking. Act out your content through your body, your eyes and face. If you are giving your audience important information that will have a positive impact on their lives, tell them with your arms, hands and facial expressions. Watch your facial expressions change as you silently articulate your presentation. Try expressing yourself using only your eyes. This will provide you with an experience of what your audience will see during your presentation.

Remember, people look at the package. You can get away with one or two weak elements, if other elements are strong. Here is where you go back and look at your priorities and perhaps update them again as you learn which things are important to you.

Listen to the Advice of Friends

A friend of mine was a candidate for political office. He had everything in the world going for him. Everything, that is, except for a rather high pitched voice. I suggested that he needed vocal training, but he did not get enough of it.

After a while, even your friends won't tell you more than once what you need. This is where listening comes in. Sometimes, when your friends tell you something that is difficult for them to say, they say it again in a quiet voice—but if you're not a good listener, you lose the chance to learn something useful. Often, they won't say it again and you will have missed the chance to improve yourself.

You have put yourself together from a clothing and cosmetics point of view. You've done the best you can based on your priorities. You've made a conscious decision to improve your vocabulary, to watch your grammar, and you've either decided that your voice is good enough or you have sought professional assistance. You've checked out your content and you've rehearsed with others if necessary. You've looked within yourself to find those things that give you confidence *and you're ready to try them out.*

Confidence is really an internal matter. If you have it, other people will see it; if you lack it, other people can spot it.

When people feel uneasy around pets, the pet will pick up on that. This is why certain animals, like cats, will go over to the person who is afraid of cats and sit next to him. People are the same; they do tend to recognize, and, in some cases even prey upon, weakness. Therefore, *don't show your weakness.*

In your final stages of preparation, remember what I said earlier: you only have one life. You do the best you can, and if people don't appreciate you, find people or situations where you can be appreciated. Don't spend a lot of time trying to win people over who don't like you. It's just a waste of time. There will always be people who, for whatever reason, don't like you. *Invest your time and energy with people you like and who like you.*

So, as you make the final adjustments to your presentation, remember that the most you can do is your best.

KNOW THE GROUND RULES

One of the most important parts of making a presentation is your decision to make that presentation. If you are asked to make a presentation by someone else, make sure you know the ground rules before you start to prepare.

In most situations, the ground rules are everything. For instance, when a person asks you come to his office and you respond by saying, "I'd rather have the presentation in my own office," this gives you an advantage. One of the most important basic rules is to choose a meeting venue in which you are most comfortable. If, however, you have the materials and samples, and you find yourself at a disadvantage at the venue where you're scheduled to present, try to change that venue. Every performer knows this. There are certain places where an entertainer goes over very well with the audience, and certain places where they don't. If a performer has a good manager, it is the job of that manager to make sure that their client only performs where he will do his best.

Remember, you want to give yourself as many advantages as possible. In this example, that means requesting a meeting at your chosen venue.

The Need to Say "No"

Many years ago, I was managing someone who had an invitation to appear on The David Letterman Show. *At the time,* The David Letterman Show *was at its peak. However, I did not let this person go on the show because, back then, David Letterman was known for being a loose cannon and I was afraid that he might make fun of the individual I was managing.*

You could say that I gave up an opportunity for my client to receive exposure on national television because I thought it was too risky. On the other hand, there were other talk show hosts who always made their guests look good, and I went with one of them, instead.

Again, before you put your materials together and make your presentation be sure that you're in a venue in which you are comfortable.

You don't always have a choice if you work for somebody and they ask you to make a presentation. But if you are assigned a location that doesn't work for you, make your superiors aware that you feel you will be at a disadvantage if you are forced to present there. They may find someone else to present, or change the venue for you. Remember, your whole team is on the same side so the whole team has a behavioral objective to win.

It would be best if, after you've established the ground rules, you could feel comfortable in any situation. That may take time and training, but rules help.

So you always want to express yourself with ease, accuracy and clarity. If people don't know what you're talking about they tend to tune you out. If they tune you out, your presentation is gone.

When you're participating in a discussion always try to keep your comments positive. Nobody wants to hear negative things. If there is something dramatically wrong in your company and you are part of a team, bring that up to your superior privately. Do not do that in public. Never make your boss look bad.

By being constructive, you can enhance someone else's presentation and become part of the team and make a friend. Rivalries and competitive atmospheres of negativity are not the kind of associations that you want to keep. Some time, somewhere, if they turn on everyone else, they will end up turning on you. Never take satisfaction that someone you don't like is unfairly treated by management. If something is unfair or a system is unfair, eventually it will get back to you.

An Uncertain Marketplace

In the present marketplace, where we are all dealing with so much uncertainty, being positive is going to be one of your most powerful tools. Find a positive way to deliver even the most negative information. Blame, criticism and negative judgments rarely lead to positive end results. Why? Making others look bad simply makes you look bad. No one wins by humiliating another person; your audience will always take the other person's side, and you will alienate them.

At this point, you've assembled the visual aids, flip charts and your slide presentation. You've calmed yourself down, found the right venue, rehearsed your presentation, and made sure you look your best with your desired image.

Now, relax and enjoy yourself. This is your time to perform what you have practiced. You maintain the advantage over your audience: you know what you have prepared for them and they don't. You have more information about this subject than they do. You may even have clever lines stashed in your pocket about the subject, while they don't.

You've got the advantage now. This is your chance to shine.

SELF-ASSESSMENT QUESTIONS

- Do you feel confident that what you have to say is meaningful and interesting to others?
- Have you identified ways to feel comfortable during your presentation or speech?

5

Your
WRITING SKILLS,
Improved
Getting the Message Across

"The medium is the message."
—MARSHALL MCLUHAN
*Educator and Author of the breakthrough text in media
theory,* Understanding Media: The Extensions of Man

In this chapter we are going to concentrate on the basic tools that are needed to improve your writing ability. Whether it's in the workplace or your life in general, the principles of good writing are the same. And the key ingredient of good writing—just like good public speaking—is content.

Unless you have something to say, don't bother writing. You're just wasting other people's time.

Writing, like speaking, is just another form of communication. The most basic rule when sharing information with others is to convey something you believe in. Therefore, any of the steps and procedures that I talk about here have absolutely no meaning if your writing does not communicate something of value. People can study the most flowery language in the world and write endless prose, but unless there is some thought behind the words, the effect will be sophomoric at best.

Regardless of which medium you choose, you must organize your writing carefully. In *The Business Writer's Handbook*, authors Gerald J. Alred, Charles T. Brusaw and Walter E. Oliu emphasize that "the best way to ensure that your writing will succeed—whether it is in the form of a memo, a resume, a proposal, or a Web page—is to approach writing using the following steps:

1. Preparation
2. Research
3. Organization
4. Writing
5. Revision

You will very likely need to follow those steps consciously—even self-consciously—at first . . . the easiest and most efficient way to write effectively is to do it systematically."

GET YOUR THOUGHTS ORGANIZED

If you have something of value to communicate, it will be difficult to get your point across unless you use the principles and techniques of effective writing. Today, there are many software programs available to help you organize your thoughts. So, one of the first things to consider is what format you want to use. Programs like Microsoft Word® and PowerPoint enable you to organize your thoughts by creating a series of bullets. If you are looking to communicate a rather complex idea, PowerPoint in particular is extremely helpful. Though *you* might know what you're talking about, PowerPoint helps the reader by breaking down difficult concepts into clearly stated units of information. PowerPoint should be reserved for more complicated presentations.

Just as Marshall McLuhan said many years ago, "the medium is the message."

Today we have many choices of media. We can write simple documents, we can use e-mail, blogs, presentations, or we can use speech. Choosing which medium to use is your first decision. For most of us, "writing" doesn't always mean putting something on paper. It can mean sending a text message, an e-mail or a faxed document.

There are many reasons why people put things in writing. One is the famous corporate strategy of "letters to the file." People often put things in writing not just for communication but to protect themselves and establish a record.

There may be times when you need to write something down in order to create a record. In these cases, although the content may not be original, your writing is still valuable.

It's an important technique to write "letters to the file" even if you don't send them to the other party. These letters act as a written record at a certain point in time of *your* version of an incident or your interpretation of a policy. If you have a letter on file or a written record, this can protect you as well as help you plan effectively the next time around.

THE IMPORTANCE OF KEEPING YOUR PERSONAL WRITING STYLE

Obviously, when you write letters to yourself, grammar, punctuation and other tools of writing are not as important as communicating the content concisely. In fact, this is true in most writing. Unless you're a famous author with a unique style of writing, the purpose of writing is to communicate your ideas as effectively as possible. Each person has a different way of communicating, and while this chapter will deal with specific techniques for writing, it's important not to lose your individual style.

A Bad Grade—on a Top Ten Hit

So many famous writers over the years would have received bad grades if their writing was graded by an English teacher. One famous songwriter and performer received a C grade at a prestigious Ivy League university for an assignment— which became a song that turned into a Top Ten Hit. English teachers, like music teachers, are there to teach you the basic principles: an English teacher instructs students in proper grammar, spelling and sentence structure. But individuals with a powerful message can become successful, and it doesn't always matter if their words are grammatically correct.

However, just as beauty is in the eyes of the beholder, so is good writing. For most people who do not have a particularly great style of writing, the fundamentals are important. This is true in fact for everyone. Even if you're going to break the rules, it's not a bad idea to learn them before you break them. If you do end up changing the rules, you will do so because of your personal style—not because you're ignorant.

CHOOSING THE RIGHT FORMAT

E-mail has become one of the most common forms of communication. It's easy to use, doesn't take much time on the part of the recipient or the sender, and is great for verifying dates, places and other specifics. The problem with e-mail is that it lacks the formality of a letter, memo or report. If you are looking to get across an idea that is somewhat complex or are dealing with a sensitive matter, then an e-mail is probably the wrong format.

Also, although e-mail is an easy way to communicate, it does not allow you to get immediate feedback from the other person. Witnessing somebody's response, listening and maintaining eye contact, and all the other basic rules of good conversation skills are completely lost when you write in e-mail. Many people think of e-mail as a two-way communication, but, in point of fact, it is not. *E-mails are a series of one-way communications that happen with such rapidity that they appear to be two-way communications.* This is very important to remember because, when relationships are going well, e-mail is fine to use. But if things are not going well, e-mail could make them deteriorate further—very quickly.

It is easier to tell somebody in an e-mail that you no longer want to do business with them than it is to do it in person or on the telephone. If you just want to get rid of somebody, e-mail may be a very effective way to do that. But things can go from very hot to cold in e-mail communications because they are essentially one-way communications—not interactive, two-way communications.

For this reason I use e-mail primarily as a means of communicating positive things. If I want to turn a situation around or I'm fighting to make a point, I try to use an approach where I can get feedback. Remember, writing is a form of communication that is intrinsically one-way.

Two-way communication is always preferable when there is a problem that you want to solve.

Advice from Experts

TIPS FOR SUCCESSFUL BUSINESS E-MAIL

Get to the point. Don't drag out or make your message too long. There is a greater chance of the recipient just skimming through it or deleting it all together.

If you are replying to an e-mail, answer all questions asked. If you don't answer all of the sender's questions in the original e-mail, rest assured you'll most likely receive more e-mails regarding the questions you left unanswered.

Fill in the subject line. Use a subject line that is meaningful to the recipient. This will insure it gets the attention you are seeking.

Use correct spelling, punctuation and grammar. Bad punctuation will not only make your e-mail hard to read, but may also change the meaning of your text, too. Run a spell checker and re-read your message before you send it. Avoid using shorthand and other personal elements. NEVER USE ALL CAPS or no caps. Proper case is essential.

Keep it on subject. In business, communication is key. Lost messages can cause a missed meeting, deadline, or have another negative impact. Don't bury a new thought in an old message. Start a new thread.

PUTTING IT TOGETHER IN A LETTER

The letter is a form of communication that can be used to show respect, to formalize a discussion or to communicate with someone. Just as you are judged on your appearance or your speech, you will be judged more on a letter than you would on an e-mail or text coming from a BlackBerry.® A letter to a person says a lot about you. It shows your level of education, your style and your thought processes.

If something is important enough to write in a letter, take the time to make sure that that letter reflects the best you have to offer. Letters can be saved, they can be used as evidence, and they can be used against you as well as in your favor. *Don't ever put anything in a letter that you don't want everyone in the world to see.*

Timeless Art

Whenever I go to the Museum of Modern Art, because I have a personality that likes to know how something came about, I always get annoyed that they don't indicate next to the piece the length of time that it took the artist to create the work of art. I would love to know how many days went into a painting or a sculpture. But there is no speed rating next to a Picasso. This means that people see that work of art for what it is. It stands on its own.

The same applies to a letter or any other written work. No one knows how long it took you to write it. All they know is that it came from you. Therefore, you may not want to spend weeks of your time writing a letter. However, do take a reasonable amount of time to make sure the spelling is correct and that the letter reflects your very best efforts.

BUSINESS LETTER ETIQUETTE

Date and address your letter. Be sure you have spelled the recipient's name and address correctly. Make sure not to omit titles, honors or qualifications.

Consider confidentiality. Mark a letter "Confidential" or "Personal" if the letter contains sensitive or personal information that you would prefer no one but the recipient to see. If the letter you received was marked "Confidential," your reply should maintain the same level of confidentiality.

Maintain a unified tone. All business letters should have a formal style; that is, there should be a consistent, courteous, organized and clear approach. Letters should be signed personally and if the recipient is a friend, you can add a more personal comment at the end, but remember that the letter could be read or referred to by a third party.

Respond on time. If you cannot respond within five working days, an acknowledgement should be sent via mail, fax, phone or e-mail.

THE REASON FOR REPORTS

A report is different from an e-mail or letter.

The purpose of the written report is to communicate content. In today's world, people are overwhelmed with information. The Internet has put data on every kind of subject at our fingertips. Unless you have something important to say, people don't want more to learn. So when you compose a report, make sure to communicate something of value to the recipient. Also be sure to organize your thoughts for maximum effectiveness.

A report is not about making you look smart, *it's about communication.* Remember the section on behavioral objectives. Your behavioral objective in sending a report is to get the recipient of the report to understand what you have to say. Many people use reports to show that they did a lot of work or spent a great deal of time on it. More often than not, however, the recipient will appreciate your showing respect for their time by communicating information in an organized, concise way.

Organization is one of the most important things to remember in generating a good report. You want to make sure that your facts are right and your logic is intact. If your facts are wrong, even if your conclusion is correct, your report will be completely ineffective.

Check your facts, check your spelling, and check your grammar. Today this is a lot easier with programs such as Microsoft Word, which allows you to review your documents quickly. Combined with the Internet, this makes it easy to check your facts and the spelling of names of people and places. It always hurts the attainment of your goal when you find out that you made a basic mistake in your report that could have been avoided by simply checking your facts.

Advice from Experts

TIPS FOR BETTER REPORTS

Craft your thesis. Have a single, unifying message in your report, and stick with it. Don't simply imply your message.

Create an outline. Break your most important points into paragraphs that follow logically from one another, making sure all points reinforce your thesis.

Collect all relevant information. Make sure you have enough information to reinforce your key points. Also, make sure that none of the information you present contradicts your thesis.

Don't be afraid of graphics. If a concept is most easily understood with a pie chart, graph or picture, then you should include them. They can break up the monotony of paragraphs and increase interest.

Repeat your points. Most people do not have the time to read everything, but they do remember what they have been told at the beginning and the end. It may be in your best interest to provide a summary section at the beginning and a conclusion at the end.

Double-check your report. Check for style, grammar, and spelling, as well as a clear and consistent thesis.

Ask someone else to review your report. It's far more difficult to be critical of your own report than it is to let someone else give you some constructive criticism.

KNOWING YOUR AUDIENCE

When you put something on paper, knowing your audience is just as important as it is when you make a presentation. No matter whether you are speaking, writing, or presenting, it is important that you know whom you are addressing.

Always think before you write or speak. Every audience is different. You don't want to use elementary terms to present to someone who is an expert or more knowledgeable about the subject than you are. People can get very offended if somebody tells them something that they already know very clearly. Without even knowing it, you can really insult someone by presuming to instruct him in something that he introduced or did himself. Therefore, always draft the tone of the report so it speaks at the appropriate level of the person to whom you are writing.

The style of your message should also reflect the subject at hand. If the subject is serious, maintain a serious tone. This doesn't mean that a professional presentation can't be enhanced by anecdotes or amusing details. Just be sure to use your judgment before introducing a tone of levity. Know your audience.

Misreading the Audience

I ran into trouble when I went to the Grand Ol' Opry to attend the Dove Awards for Christian Contemporary Music, which was being televised live. When the master of ceremonies asked everyone in the audience to pray for high ratings, I perceived this as a joke and responded by making another joke. It grossly offended everybody I was with and was not a good idea. I didn't know the other people that well, so I shouldn't have made the joke.

If you don't know the people you're talking to, don't raise controversial subjects or make jokes that may offend them. This may seem obvious, but it's a mistake I've made often in my life. Whether it's at a job interview, or in your writing, don't discuss politics or religion if it's not necessary.

Unless it is an intrinsic part of what you are trying to present, try not to do something that could hurt you. *Remember your behavioral objectives.* Your objective is to get what you want through speaking or writing. Introducing politics, religion or other controversial elements can only hurt you. Stay away from sensitive subjects in job interviews, in discussions with people you don't know well, in presentations, or in your writing.

Too Close a Shave

A close friend of mine, Victor Kiam, who owned Remington Products and the New England Patriots, thought he was among friends when he made a sexist remark about a woman reporter in a locker room. That joke began a series of incidents that ended up bringing down his business and his career.

You never know who you're talking to, you never know who's in the room, and when you're writing, you never know where your work will end up.

On another occasion, I was invited to dinner at Victor Kiam's penthouse for a business discussion. During the visit he gave me a copy of his new book, Going for It! How to Succeed as an Entrepreneur. *When I got home and read through it, to my surprise, I discovered a chapter on how he screwed me in a business deal.*

Needless to say, his remarks and writing eventually caught up with him.

DON'T LET YOUR WORDS
COME BACK TO HAUNT YOU

Today, your writing is likely to be read and edited by other people. Be careful that the editors don't take away from your meaning. But also make sure that editors don't take away your style. Editors can also help make corrections that need to be made. Don't take the changes personally, and if they are of value, use them. But if editors take away from your meaning or your style, feel free to reject their changes. If your name is on a report or document, make sure it conveys what you mean.

In the current environment, written documents can help you, but they can also be used against you. Make sure that when you commit something to writing, it is true and expresses what you believe. *Unless there is a specific reason for it, make sure that you don't commit something to writing that could prove to be controversial in later years.* This is not to say that any writer should compromise their convictions. If possible however, it's best to avoid controversy, so resist the temptation to include information that is not necessary to make your case or that could hurt you in the future.

From Cocktail Party to Controversy

In the 1950s, many people faced repercussions because they went to parties, had drinks with, or conversed and socialized with people who were associated with the Communist Party. Remember that during that period of time, although Russia had been our ally in the Second World War, the Cold War was in progress. The McCarthy era fostered paranoia, which meant that many people who were perfectly innocent were nonetheless held accountable for behavior that seemed suspicious—even if all they did was have a certain kind of conversation at a cocktail party. It resulted in their being black-listed and ostracized.

Try to stay away from politics, religion, and other hot topics in your writing and conversation, unless that is a part of who you are. If the subject is of real importance to you, then go with your convictions, but know that anything you say or write may not remain private.

Watching what you write and say is particularly important in this age of the Internet with web sites like YouTube which can preserve the smallest things that you do or say. *You don't want to find that 20 years from now something that you added to a report as a sidebar comes back to destroy your political or professional future.* It might have been said as a joke or an offhand remark at the time, but it can come back to haunt you. So avoid it.

Google saves virtually every single e-mail that is written through their system. The government of the United States records tens of millions of conversations and e-mails and could subpoena all kinds of information if necessary. People mistakenly think that when they erase something from their computer, it is gone. This is not the case. Computers retain almost all the information that was ever written on them.

You should be especially careful about correspondence in the workplace. Employers often have much more information about their employees than their employees ever know. Don't ever send an e-mail with any negative or damaging information. Every e-mail that you write in the office becomes the property of your employer, and they have the right to review anything you've written, at any time.

We live in a time when information is of the greatest importance to mankind, but also at a time when the most minute bit of information can be brought up years later and used against the writer.

Writing is an important tool, since it defines you and can enhance you. . . but it can also injure you. In medicine there is a saying that any drug that can cure can also harm. That is also the case with writing.

SELF-ASSESSMENT QUESTIONS

- Do you feel you have a personal writing style? What does it communicate?
- Do you focus on your objective when writing? How often do you feel that you obtain that objective?

6

Your
CRITICAL THINKING SKILLS,
Improved
Strategies for Problem Solving,
Negotiation and Conflict Resolution

"Chance favors only the prepared mind."
—LOUIS PASTEUR
World Renowned French Chemist
and Microbiologist

Decision-making is one of the most personal areas that you will encounter in business or personal situations. There are no easy answers as to how people arrive at their decisions. Sometimes you go to movie and you say, "Who decided to make a movie about *that*?" Or you may look at a dress and say, "Who decided to make *that*?" At the end of the day, whether you like the end result or not, someone is behind every decision.

Every action begins as a decision. Yet, though we all make decisions, *most of us don't give much thought as to how we arrived at them.* This chapter will guide you through a systematic, organized way of making decisions.

LOOK AT THE EVIDENCE

Sometimes, people look at the facts, and based on their experiences, arrive at a decision. On other occasions, they make decisions by following the instructions of a superior or authority figure.

For example, some people look to God for answers.

In the United States, our system of justice is designed to produce a decision—a verdict—based on evidence. During a trial, prosecutors and defense attorneys each present the evidence, which is meant to form a logical, cohesive picture of what events took place surrounding a crime so that a jury can decide if the defendant is innocent or guilty.

Ideally, a jury would make a decision based on the logical arguments presented during the trial. However, members of the jury can also make decisions based on something as simple as the appearance of the defendant or their own personal intuition as to whether or not they think the defendant is guilty.

Lawyers want individuals on the jury who will make a decision based on the information presented at the trial. It is precisely for this reason that prosecutors and defense attorneys participate in jury selection. During jury selection, the lawyers interview potential jurors to try to eliminate those people who they believe will, for whatever reason, decide either for or against a defendant based on anything other than the factual evidence presented.

THE SCIENCE OF DECISION-MAKING

The scientific method was developed specifically to provide people with a systematic, organized way of making decisions. *The SELF, Improved* aims to do just that by making a science out of behaviors, actions, and impressions in your life that might otherwise be subjective.

What makes science, science? *Science is a process by which we generate hypotheses and then proceed to prove them either true or false.* For example, if we see a red hot piece of metal, we generate an instant hypothesis that the metal is hot. Then, we may either touch the metal or approach it with caution to determine whether our hypothesis is correct. Over time, we stop making hypotheses and confirming every single detail of an experience that we come across. Instead, we start to make educated guesses based on past experience: we make generalizations and assumptions.

These generalizations and assumptions help us make decisions promptly and efficiently so we can get through life. However, this method can also lead to mistakes.

A WORD ABOUT GENERALIZATIONS

Generalizations can sometimes lead to catastrophe if we assume that systems are correct and in working order without double-checking them. *You certainly wouldn't want an airplane pilot not to check his instruments because he had made the generalization that, because his instruments usually work, that he could skip it.*

Generalizations can also become discriminatory when made about people. This occurs when we use one experience with a certain person as the basis for judging an entire group of people. This is a mistake. Hopefully no one would adopt that type of hypothesis or, if they did, they would challenge that assumption rather than decide not to interact with someone based on a generalization.

Decision-making of a subjective nature, as well as an objective nature, can be valuable in certain situations. While we always want as much information as possible before making a decision, in certain circumstances there may not be enough time for this.

For example, disaster medical personnel make decisions all the time as to who is most important to treat first and who can be treated later. These decisions, like all decisions, are not always right.

Sometimes, though, when there is very little time to decide, a choice must be made immediately.

DEDUCTIVE REASONING

Deductive reasoning is defined as taking a series of facts, looking at them carefully, and based on these actual facts, coming to a conclusion. *Inductive reasoning* takes place when we look at a series of facts and use our own life experiences to form our conclusions. With inductive reasoning, we make a decision based on how our mind sees what's around us. Both inductive and deductive reasoning play important roles in the world. While *deductive* reasoning is considered to be more logical, *inductive* reasoning has led to some of the greatest discoveries and inventions of our time.

Generally, decisions made through deductive reasoning do not allow for big, new ideas to be generated: that is usually the domain of inductive reasoning.

TAKING STEPS TO MAKE A DECISION

"Even if you are on the right track, you will get run over if you just sit there."

—WILL ROGERS
Vaudeville and Early Motion Picture Actor,
Humorist and Columnist

Perhaps some of this may seem a bit philosophical for day-to-day decision-making. In making day-to-day decisions, it is generally a good approach *to look at the facts* or the body of evidence in front of you, *use your experience*, and then *make a decision*.

Separation of Church and State

One of the reasons why the Founding Fathers separated church and state when drafting the Constitution was that they did not want decisions of government in the United States to be made based upon religious beliefs. They believed that doing so would violate the principles upon which they wanted the new country founded. Today, the President nominates and Congress appoints judges to the Supreme Court based in part on their personal beliefs. That means we know how they will vote on certain issues, irrespective of the evidence. In effect, the highest court in the land is not an impartial tribunal.

Paradoxically, in most companies, it is illegal to make decisions based upon various types of discrimination. This is stated in almost all the job manuals and many employees have to sign off on this. However, it is virtually impossible to enforce this. This is one of the reasons why we talked about knowing how to dress and managing your personal appearance so you can convey the impression you want when you go for a job interview or a meeting.

How do we attain greater clarity in making decisions? Well, the first thing to do is to gain as much knowledge about the matter as possible. You can call on your own educational base, but with the availability of the Internet, you can get valuable general information on almost anything. You never know what might be out there that might help you.

Next, no matter how you gather information, when faced with a decision, break it into its various elements. Find out what the issue consists of. Determine the consequences at stake. Then use logic and experience to make your choice, while remaining aware of the consequences of your decision—and the consequences of indecision.

Sometimes people think that by putting off a decision they are putting off the problem. Indecision is also a decision: it is a decision *not* to decide.

Waiting on a Ruling

In the judicial system, an individual in jail can file a petition before the judge. The judge can delay making a ruling. While the judge puts off the ruling, the inmate waits in prison. In effect, the judge has decided not to make a decision. In fact, the judge's indecision has consequences: the inmate has to wait in jail.

No matter the situation, being indecisive always has an effect. Remember, not making a decision doesn't get you off the hook.

BECOMING A BETTER NEGOTIATOR

"Life is a series of negotiations, and so are relationships and friendships and marriage and family interactions— just about every other aspect of living involves negotiating at one time or another."

—FREDERIC FLACH, MD, AUTHOR
Resilience: Discovering a New Strength at Times of Stress

What are the elements of negotiation? What makes a good negotiator? How do you become a good negotiator? Negotiation is just another very specific form of interaction. In a negotiation, you're trying to find a compromise and come to an agreement that is acceptable to the person you are dealing with, either for yourself or the person you're representing.

KNOW WHAT *YOU* WANT

The key element in a negotiation is the identification of your behavioral objectives in the negotiation. What is it that you want?

If you don't know what you want, you can't be a good negotiator. If you know what you want, you're off to a good start. Now being a good negotiator is a little bit like establishing your priority list at the beginning of this book. You have to weigh various factors: you not only have to know what you want and absolutely need, but you also have to know what you're willing to give up because you can trade with what you don't care about. You also need to know the other side.

KNOW WHAT *THEY* WANT

You need to understand the other side's point of view. *The failure to understand the other side's point of view is the number one problem in all negotiations.* Among other things, it can lead to bringing up the wrong things at the wrong time.

Think Before You Ask

If the company is losing money, it's bad timing and bad form to ask for a raise. I once had an employee meet me at a restaurant where he asked me for a raise. I told him that his division had been losing money for the last year. He asked me what that had to do with him or his raise. That was the end of his job.

MEET THEM HALFWAY

If you don't care about the other side of things; that is, if you don't care about the party you are negotiating with, you will never be a good negotiator. Good negotiators listen and watch while they and their counterparts talk. They look for what they need, and they try to determine what the other side will, or will not give up.

Most people who are in negotiation are in it because they want to settle the issue. Otherwise, they would not be negotiating. That means that by the time you get to a negotiation, you're already halfway there. *Meet the other person halfway and do all that you can to see their side of things.*

Too often people consider negotiation as an equation where each point is looked at as if one side wins and, in that process, the other side loses something. This myopic vision prevents the most important outcome of a negotiation, namely: a win-win situation. If you can provide something that you may enjoy doing or want to do that helps the other side, they, in turn may be more appreciative, resulting in a win for both sides.

DON'T NEGOTIATE AGAINST YOURSELF

When negotiating, you need to be sure you know who has the power to make a decision when you go into the negotiation.

Let's say that you do have the power to make a decision. The worst thing you can do is try to negotiate with someone who does *not* have the power to make a decision. *This is called negotiating against yourself.*

It's negotiating against yourself because, if the two of you agree on something, the other party can come back after the fact and say that they actually need someone else's approval before agreeing. In this way, they are essentially negating what they just promised, whereas you are bound by anything that you have said. If you do find yourself in this kind of situation, let go of your sole decision-making role. In other words, back off and state that you, too, need another person or authority to give final approval.

A Good Technique

Over the course of my life, I have been a member of several Boards. I often maintained a certain degree of control over many of the Boards. However, I always gave myself a way out by saying that I couldn't do anything without Board approval. This gave me a way to back out, in case the other side changed something.

A word of caution: don't abuse this technique, or eventually people will cease doing business with you because they will view it as bad faith. Nonetheless, this is a very effective tactic when used responsibly.

NEGOTIATING CONTRACTS

There are instances, when negotiating a contract, where you want to look for one powerful clause that will give you a tremendous amount of control. I call this a *control sentence*. If you have a control sentence in a negotiated contract that negates the rest of the contract, don't show your hand—just do the deal.

Advice from Experts

IMPORTANT REMINDERS FOR NEGOTIATIONS

Know what you are after. Define what you want clearly. Prepare by stating your goals in your own mind and be ready to share them with the person with whom you are negotiating.

Know what you are talking about. Be sure to do your homework.

De-personalize the negotiation as much as you can. Don't link your self-esteem with winning or losing or reaching closure. Don't take the results personally.

Be prepared *not* to get what you want, or not all of what you want. Being aware of the possibility that you might not get what you are after gives you an important edge, since this way you are prepared to "lose." Knowing how to lose is a vital part of being a successful negotiator.

Be forthright and honest. Be honest, but don't reveal all your cards too soon. You want to wait until the right moment to introduce the knowledge you, and you alone, have. This knowledge can turn the argument around.

Keep an open mind about the outcome. If things don't go as you planned, keep in mind that a negotiation that fails can sometimes provide a valuable window of opportunity. This opportunity will often be one you never would have imagined, and one that can be more profitable and meaningful to you in the end.

For example, employers might put in contracts with employees that they have the right to terminate the agreement with or without cause. Hollywood contracts were famous for their "morals clause" which gave the studios enormous power over the actors.

Remember this even if you are negotiating a contract with friends. After all, the next time you go back to review the terms of the contract, it will probably be because something has gone wrong. If things do go wrong, you want to have a *control sentence* to which you can turn.

HANDLING CONFLICTS

When dealing with conflicts, the most important thing is to understand everybody's side of the argument. There's an old saying that states, there are only two sides to every argument. But it can be more complex than that.

Six Sides to Every Argument

I had a friend who brokered many business deals. My friends always say that, before they met him, they used to think there were two sides to every argument. Then, after knowing him, they realized there were six sides. Business negotiations often involve brokers, finders, and other intermediaries who have their own interests as well, in addition to the interests of the two principals.

No matter how many sides there are to an argument, it is important to be sure you understand *all* perspectives.

TYPES OF CONFLICTS

Because there are many different sides to an argument, there are several different types of conflicts.

One type of conflict occurs when everybody is of good will and the conflict occurs only because people see things differently. In this type of situation, resolution of the conflict is generally easy. It basically involves trying to get one person to see the other side's position. Then, both parties will either agree, or agree to disagree.

Another type of conflict occurs when people have a specific objective and don't really care about what's right or wrong. A good person to resolve this type of conflict is an extremely logical individual, one who can go step-by-step through the process and, to the extent possible, use deductive rather than inductive reasoning. Utilizing deductive reasoning in this way will ensure that things remain logical, and that third parties don't bring in their own subjectivities—that is, their own opinions.

Doing so would ruin any chance of resolution.

EXTREME CONFLICT RESOLUTION: "TALK THEM DOWN"

In a conflict where somebody is clearly wrong, or even psychologically unbalanced, it is the job of the conflict resolver to talk down the person who is causing the conflict.

A hostage negotiator often has to walk into a situation where he has absolutely no idea what is bothering the person who took the hostages. Yet, he has to get the hostages released by talking the hostage-taker down. How does he accomplish this? He does this by trying to find some way to relate to the person who is causing the conflict.

This strategy really isn't too different from what I talked about in the section on job interviews: during a job interview, you gain an edge by finding a common ground with the interviewer, whatever that ground may be.

Obviously, in the case of a hostage negotiator, logic and deductive reasoning are not going to go very far with a mentally unstable person. But you can learn from this example: in conflict resolution, you've got to try to find out what the other person wants, and then ascertain how you can possibly deliver it.

Most of us don't face life-and-death situations like hostage negotiation on the job every day. But we do have problems that come up that need to be resolved in some way, so we need to do what's possible.

THE POINT OF NO RETURN

"I've had a few arguments with people, but I never carry a grudge. You know why? While you're carrying a grudge, they're out dancing."

—BUDDY HACKETT
Legendary Comedian and Actor

Reaching the point-of-no-return in an argument means that things have been said that cannot be taken back, even after the conflict has been resolved. This happens in marriages, business situations, and friendships. Somebody gets mad, says something that offends somebody else, and the other person, instead of responding in a deliberate and logical way, reacts emotionally. Often, this emotional reaction means that the other person, too, will say something hurtful. The end result is that the relationship between the parties is severely damaged and, sometimes, permanently destroyed.

This is always a stupid way to end a relationship.

Control your actions, be deliberate, and if you really want to separate and end a relationship, do so on your own terms and in a way that is also responsible and respectful.

Staying in Control

I was recently at a meeting where I suddenly and very clearly realized that I was not going to do business with the party I was interviewing. The other party consisted of friends of a friend, and I didn't just want to just say, "I don't want to do business with you."

So I waited until they said something potentially offensive, towards the end of the meeting, and said I was too offended to continue the meeting. Remember the saying, "Her ad lib lines were well rehearsed." If you're the professional and you've learned the professional tools, you control the situation. You do things on your own ground and in your own time.

PROBLEM SOLVING SKILLS

Problem solving involves many of the same steps as decision-making. In order to solve a problem, you use the tools of deductive and inductive reasoning. These tools, combined with your experience, help you make a decision.

Problem solving, unlike usual decision-making, often raises an issue of the unknown. *A problem is basically a question to be considered, solved, or answered.*

BREAK IT INTO PARTS

Look at a problem as you would a mathematical equation: view it from all sides and size it up. If it is complex, break it into its parts. Usually, when a problem is broken down to its parts, it becomes easier to solve. The tools that you're using in the Science of Self-Improvement to assess yourself and slowly change in order to accomplish your goals are the same tools that you can use in solving almost any kind of problem. You look at its various components and assign an importance rating or weight to each of the components that will provide a priority-based approach to tackling the problem.

As previously stated in the Introduction, while a lot of people do this from a subjective point of view, writing down your priorities helps you visualize your goals. The numbers will help you turn qualitative information into quantitative information that you can use in your everyday life.

For example, someone may be wondering whether to stay in a relationship or not, or whether to leave a job or not. Initially, these problems seem very big. When you break them into their components, the questions become simpler, and become elements that you can work on.

With every problem comes questions. If you are in a position where you don't know whether to leave a job or relationship, you can ask yourself: *What am I looking for? What do I want? Does this job or that person supply it?*

Problem solving is just reducing complex issues to simple parts and solving them.

SELF-ASSESSMENT QUESTIONS

- Do you make good decisions?
- Do you feel comfortable and skilled at negotiating with people who don't agree with you?
- Do you think through your choices? Do you identify your desired outcomes?
- Do you make generalizations about your world or do you use specifics to evaluate your experiences?

7

Your
INTERPERSONAL SKILLS,
Improved
Discover the Power of People

"When people talk, listen completely. Most people
never listen."
—Ernest Hemingway
*American Writer and Journalist, Pulitzer Prize and
Nobel Prize in Literature Winner*

Interaction with others is what your charts and work on the
Science of Self-Improvement leads to. Some of the concepts
in this chapter will of necessity seem redundant or very similar
to the material covered in the chapters on communication. This
is because most of the techniques of *The SELF, Improved* are very
similar but just vary slightly when they are adapted to different
situations.

Although we live in a world where communicating on the phone,
over the Internet, through BlackBerrys® and other handheld
devices is becoming more and more common, it is important
to remember that *interacting face to face is still the most powerful
means of communicating with someone.*

COMMUNICATION SKILLS, IMPROVED

An effective communicator not only expresses what he or she is thinking, but also has an understanding of what is on the minds of others. Essentially, an effective communicator can successfully convey information to others about what they want.

Nobody can be an effective communicator if you are not interesting to the person with whom you are interacting. Otherwise, *the other person will tune you out.*

There are, of course, exceptions, such as when someone is the boss and people have to listen to him (or her). Even if this is the case, however, if a boss' style of communication is based only on the fact that people *have* to listen to him, ultimately, he's not going to be a very good boss or a leader.

Some say leaders are born, not made. It is true that some people are born leaders and possess a certain charisma; however, everyone can be trained to be better than they are, no matter how they may have started out. It is just as I said in previous chapters: you have the advantage, if you are prepared.

Remember Louis Pasteur's words: *"Chance favors only the prepared mind."* In other words, while you may get lucky, your chances of getting lucky are dramatically increased *if you are prepared.*

Knowing how to be prepared is the purpose of this book.

Politics and the Power of Persuasion
by The Hon. Michael Balboni
Former New York State Senator
Former "Homeland Security Czar" for New York State

Throughout my career, I have had to constantly deal with the question, "Why should I believe you? You're a politician." This is unfair because it fails to assess the person, and instead adopts all the negative assumptions and assertions of society and the media.

Yet "politics" and "being political" are the art of dealing with people in a way in which consensus can be achieved, leadership assented to, and an affirmation through the ballot box be realized. Aren't these outcomes similar to those in the business arena?

Politics is people management. Good politics results in the empowering of colleagues, the inspiration of partners and the encouragement of perhaps complete strangers in your ability to perform the task at hand. Politics enables achievement without unnecessary confrontation. The willingness to submit your will to that of another in order to succeed in a longer-range goal is a fundamental skill set needed to "be political." The negative connotation comes from the cynical use of politics to simply achieve power without regard to the people it affects.

The key is to adopt the aspects of politics that make people feel good about themselves and you, without compromising their interests. There are several traits which can smooth the way to cooperation. These are not new techniques, and have been utilized throughout human history. Nonetheless, they are very effective, particularly in today's world in which people have encased themselves in a technological cocoon, texting endlessly and isolating themselves from broad human interaction. Below are some strategies which will lead to more effective "political" interactions.

Focus—Politics is about people and how to communicate with them. The most precious thing you can do is to give people your full attention, preventing yourself from being distracted by phone calls, e-mails, or other people. Former President Bill Clinton is a master of this. By giving you his undivided attention, he makes you feel like you are the most important person in the world. You may disagree with what he is saying, but you want to listen to him because you feel he wants to listen to you. In our multi-tasking world, however, we have all lost the focus on one another. By simply refocusing on the person, we give ourselves the opportunity to reconnect in significant and meaningful ways.

Preparation—When we first meet someone, we approach them as a blank piece of paper. We wait for them to tell us what they want, feel, desire or think. Yet, if we spend the time to research with whom we are meeting, we will be able to anticipate what that person needs, wants and desires, and this will put you in the position to craft an answer or response ahead of time, while demonstrating to the listener that you empathize with them and their problems. Before I meet someone for the first time, I use search engines to provide me with my "due diligence" about the person. Given the ease of programs like Google, there is really no excuse for not doing such a search. Once again, this will provide you with the best opportunity to connect with the person whom you are dealing with.

Language—There are all sorts of books that describe the use of language as a way of forming a quick and useful bond with the people you interact with. My rule of thumb is to avoid any confrontational language until I absolutely have to make a decision. In this, I try to utilize some "verbal judo"; I take the concern or intent and turn it around so that the person is more secure and comfortable. It is virtually impossible to reach an agreement with someone if they are defensive, angry or threatened. I am not suggesting that a false façade of caring be adopted, but rather, if you can create a passive, inviting environment for the person you are speaking to, once again, the opportunity for agreement is maximized. The trap, of course, is that you will be perceived as being insincere. In order to effectively communicate, you have to want to do it and care about the affect your words will have on the person to whom you are speaking. If you are perceived as being insincere, you will poison the relationship instead of enabling it.

These three strategies can never take the place of hard work, honesty and innovation. But, if used properly, these skills will create the maximum environment for success. The bottom line is that you can tell someone the secrets of life, but if they don't want to listen to you, you might as well have said nothing. The above strategies will be your best tools for making certain that your message is heard.

KNOW THE CONTEXT

Before you even say or communicate anything, *take the time to understand where the other party is coming from.* The context in which you are speaking or interacting may dominate what you have to say. For example, many comedians decided not to perform immediately following 9/11. They figured that it would be inappropriate or impossible to be funny in that context.

Behaving Inappropriately in the Public Eye

I actually went to a funeral in which a United States Senator dropped in to pay his condolences and started waving to his constituents. I'll always remember how inappropriate and how out of place he was.

REMEMBER: IT'S A SMALL WORLD

Always consider the context before communicating with others.

A Small World

We do live in a very small world. I learned this during a meeting with several people, including a business manager who represented the baseball players Hank Aaron and the late Roberto Clemente. Myself, the business manager, and others involved in the deal began the meeting by having some drinks and chatting casually.

During the conversation, the manager asked one of my partners where she lived. She mentioned a town in Westchester, New York, to which the business manager replied, "I lived around there, too." My business partner asked for his previous address, as she knew the area well. He gave an address, which she surprisingly remarked had been her old address, as well.

This simple exchange quickly and unexpectedly ignited an uncontrollable episode of crying and screaming. It turned out that this woman had bought the business manager's house with her mother who had died due to an illness resulting from toxic ingredients in the soil surrounding the house. As a matter of fact, this woman had been trying to locate the previous owner by name to discuss this tragic event.

At this point, it did no good for anyone to try to change the subject, and, obviously, this meeting did not end well.

It's unlikely that you'll be in a situation where so much goes out of your control so quickly, as it did in the example above. Furthermore, talking about where you live and where you were raised generally will not lead to conflict. Use the example above as a reminder of how important it is to *keep the conversation focused on your objective.*

FOCUS ON YOUR OBJECTIVES

Remember your behavioral objectives. If non-necessary conversation is controversial, forget it. Remain on target and keep the discussion focused on the subject matter.

When you interact with people during a meeting or a discussion, you want to know how they feel about you, how they feel about their circumstances, and how they feel about the subject matter that you're about to discuss.

If they're on your side, this will make your job a lot easier and you can be friendly, even jovial, and have a good time. If, on the other hand, you know they are going to dislike what you have to say, you should be very careful.

Do not say anything that you're unprepared for. It's almost like talking to an investigator when you're a suspect. Just assume anything that you say can and will be used against you. It's always amazing how many people think that they can wing it with police or investigators. Never say anything without a professional present. She may have done nothing wrong but even lying to investigators is against the law, as Martha Stewart found out. The same thing with social interactions. Always over-prepare for every situation to be sure your arguments are fully supported. You don't get beaten by overestimating your opponent. You lose when you underestimate your opponent.

Prepare yourself by researching and anticipating, as best you can, their response to the subject matter.

Now, aside from protecting yourself, the other reason for understanding how people feel is that you have to get beyond the blinders that everybody wears. Everybody has hot buttons, everybody has something that they stand for. If you press the wrong buttons they are going to tune you out. They won't even hear anything positive that you have to say.

Playing Politics

I never really understood why a President's position on abortion was so important to that office. The President doesn't deal with the abortion issue on a day-to-day basis, one would hope. But nevertheless, people always ask a candidate, "What is your position on abortion?" And it's always interesting to watch the politicians dance around it.

There is no upside to taking a strong position. It can—and will—alienate one part of the population or another. This is what we discussed in an earlier chapter: don't talk about politics or religion, and don't talk about highly controversial topics if they're not relevant to the discussion at hand. Just as we said that you should try to establish some commonality with the person you are meeting, you should also avoid any divisive topics that can destroy the connection you just developed. Without placing careful thought into your discussion, you may end up in a situation where you don't even know what is in store for you, and you won't be equipped to prevent the conversation from quickly going sour.

Once you can anticipate what the people you are going to interact with think about the situation and the subject you are going to introduce, you will go into the meeting or the discussion prepared and knowledgeable. As outlined in the previous chapters, you should take every other advantage you can get by dressing appropriately, listening carefully to what the other party is saying, using the other techniques of good communication, and making the right impression.

Keep your own behavioral objectives at the forefront of your mind.

Most of the time the behavioral objectives are simple: *you have an agenda and you want the other people to be on board.* You want to include them and have a policy of inclusion.

Although usually you are not going to hear many new ideas, when you do, acknowledge them, edit them, and if they're good make them part of your presentation. If not, be polite, acknowledge the contribution and then shred it in your brain and don't mention it again. Don't tell people they had a bad idea. That's never a good idea.

SET UP YOUR NEXT "SHOT"

As stated earlier, interpersonal skills are a combination of being not only a good listener, but also an *active listener*. What is an active listener? An active listener is somebody who responds to the speaker by asking a question, making eye contact, or using body language to let the other person know that they have been heard. This ensures successful interaction. After all, successful interaction takes what you want, *and what they want,* into consideration.

A bad listener is somebody who's simply waiting for the other person to stop speaking so they can say what they want to say. It doesn't show respect if, instead of listening, you are just waiting for the other person to finish so you can have your chance to speak. You witness bad listeners in debates all the time—particularly when it comes to political debates. Candidates often behave as bad listeners.

You can see the public hates this. They want opponents to show respect for one another.

Interpersonal skills are also about negotiating, asserting yourself and getting what you want. Getting what you want includes making the other person feel good. All too often, people are very shortsighted: they only want what they want at a particular meeting.

Life is like playing billiards: your shot is important, but so is leaving the cue ball where you want it for the next shot. Before and during a meeting, keep in mind that you're going to see these people again, so not only is it important that you obtain your objectives at that meeting, but it is equally vital for you to have them on your side at the conclusion as a set-up for any subsequent meeting.

So be careful to end the encounter well. Don't just ram something down their throats at the end of the meeting and force them to accept it. If asserting yourself is a primary concern for you, you can find other ways to do so, such as highlighting your intelligence, your knowledge of the subject, your manner of speaking, and your body language.

Asserting yourself by intimidating people is always a bad idea. You want these people to be your friends and supporters.

That is what leadership is all about.

BUSINESS ETIQUETTE, IMPROVED

In interacting with others in the workplace, you have to use business etiquette, just as you have to use personal etiquette in your everyday life. Business etiquette is different from personal etiquette in that it acknowledges the different roles that people have and their positions within a company.

If you are working with a multinational corporation, business etiquette can change from one culture to another.

Be Respectful

The exchanging of business cards is of great importance in the Japanese community. Japanese businessmen often hand you their business card at the beginning of a meeting with two hands and treat it as if it is a gift. If you take that card and just shove it in your pocket without looking at it, it will be considered an insult.

Even if you had entered into this situation with no clue about this culture's particular custom, if you had been attentive to the person and noted how much importance he gave to his business card and how carefully he presented it, you would have known to show that card some respect. This is part of being thoughtful. It's similar to getting a gift that you don't like from a relative. You know you will keep the gift in a closet somewhere, but every time your relative comes over, you will take it out. This is worth it for the sake of the family harmony.

If you don't have time to do the research on a certain culture's rules of business etiquette, at least be sure to carefully observe the other person's behavior so that you don't offend him. It's all in the interest of harmony.

Business etiquette is also about making someone's boss look important to the people under them, as well as making other people at the meeting look good to their bosses. Business etiquette includes the way you dress, the respect that you show to people and all of the other principles that we have gone over in this book.

A GOOD INTRODUCTION

In the book *Power Etiquette: What You Don't Know Can Kill Your Career*, Dana May Casperson emphasizes the importance of introductions. Even if you feel awkward or are unsure about whom to introduce first, be gracious and make an introduction regardless. An introduction is important because it opens the door for people to interact and get to know one another.

Casperson outlines some basic rules to keep in mind:

1. When introducing people in the office, always state the name of the more senior individual first, even if he or she is younger.
2. When introducing a co-worker to a family member, include personal information to help individuals connect.

Advice from Experts
_____

BUSINESS ETIQUETTE REMINDERS

Be on time. Punctuality shows respect. If you are running behind, have the courtesy to advise the people waiting for you.

Don't obsessively check your phone or PDA. While it is important to have access to vital communications, during important or even casual meetings, stay focused on the people in the room.

Wear appropriate attire. Dress well. Dress neatly. Dress professionally.

Watch your language. Don't use casual or inappropriate language at any time.

Have a professional handshake. When you shake hands, your grip should be strong but not crushing, and your handshake should be accompanied by direct eye contact with the person you are greeting.

Pay attention. Engage your active listening skills.

BUSINESS ETIQUETTE, DAY TO DAY

Sometimes good etiquette also involves knowing when to let something go and not take personal offense, despite the other party's actions, words or manners.

Don't Take It Personally

It's important in daily interactions not to take everything personally. Most people don't really care about you or the content of a meeting, or even what you have to say. At the end of the day, they're really just interested in getting to their own lives (and you probably are, too). So if somebody says something negative about an idea that you brought forth or about some work that you've done, don't take it personally. Instead, take a step back and look at your options. You can either defend the work if you think this person is wrong, or, if it's not important, let it go. Remember your behavioral objectives and focus on meeting those goals.

AVOID MAKING ENEMIES

Unless somebody is your superior and you think a comment from them might negatively impact your employment if it gets back to your boss, letting things die a natural death is often the best solution. If something does not directly affect your attainment of your behavioral objectives, don't waste your time or effort.

Don't engage someone and make them an enemy unless absolutely necessary. Many fights start because one person makes a comment that the other person finds to be personally insulting. Then, the listener responds with a negative comment, and, soon, the situation escalates into a conflict. *The best way to resolve any situation is not to let it get to the level of conflict.*

Be professional; remember, if you are playing with professional tools you are going to win the game. It's not important to win every point in every situation. *Save your powder for when you need it, save your energy for where it will do the most good and fight only when you must.*

NO ONE'S COUNTING YOUR LOSSES

We all have disappointments in our lives. For many of us, those disappointments may include money lost on investments, losing a job or contract, and maybe even the ending of an important relationship.

So what. No one really cares. The important thing to remember is that these disappointments are not the end of the world. You're not a baseball player; nobody is counting your losses. People only look at your successes. Unless you're a person whose life is frequently chronicled in the news, most people don't know or care about the mistakes you've made. Instead, they are more likely to take notice of what you've done right. So highlight your successes and learn from your failures.

FAILURE IS AN OPPORTUNITY

"I've missed more than 9,000 shots in my career. I've lost almost 300 games. 26 times, I've been trusted to take the game's winning shot and missed. I've failed over and over and over again in my life. And that is why I succeed."

—MICHAEL JORDAN
*Olympian, Athlete, Member of
NBA Hall of Fame and Businessman*

Failure is important to success. It teaches you what not to do, and sometimes, it even teaches you what careers not to pursue. If you have a really bad voice and they throw you out of the choir, it's better than wasting your life trying to be a singer who is never going to make it. Consider your failures a roadmap of where not to go again.

Know When to Walk Away

Casino operators know that guests at the casino will keep putting more and more money down when they are losing in the hopes that they can make it all back on a bigger bet.

They're right—the players generally don't end up as winners. The operators do.

If you're losing all the time at something, move on to something else. There are a lot of opportunities in the world. Even a relationship that has soured presents an opportunity to start a new relationship that probably has a better chance. So there's really no such thing as failure.

You can turn it around. Know when to walk away.

After all, scientists using the scientific method often move from failure to failure in their quest to find the right solution. *That's not losing—that's research.*

So don't feel disappointed if you don't succeed on your first attempt at something. Dwelling on it will only take away your enthusiasm, and will ultimately damage your confidence in your next venture. One of the reasons why I ask you to spend a lot of time on the charts and your personal priorities is that, when faced with problems, it's always best to go back to numbers.

Even if you hate math, the numbers you come up with in the assessments are an objective way of looking at where you are and where you're going. They are not judgmental.

THE IMPORTANCE OF ASKING QUESTIONS

When you hear something you don't understand, don't pretend you know what it means and keep talking. *Ask questions.*

Don't Assume

You probably know the saying, "When you assume, you make an ASS out of U and ME." This is generally true. Asking questions if you really don't know the answers is much better than assuming something and risking getting it wrong.

But don't ask questions just to look smart. People will know what you're trying to do, and they will dislike you for it.

ALWAYS BE CLEAR

Some people think that if they use complex language when they speak that they will sound intelligent. This seldom works and, more importantly, it violates a basic rule. *Our basic rule is to obtain your behavioral objectives.* If you're not clear in your communications, other people are not going to be able to follow what you want them to do, and your objectives will be obscured.

Getting others to do what you want them to do is one of your behavioral objectives in all interactions. You accomplish this by being strong in your interpersonal skills.

SELF-ASSESSMENT QUESTIONS

- Do you stay on the point of a conversation? Do you give the other person equal opportunity to voice their opinions?
- Are your image and communication techniques appropriate for the context of each specific meeting you attend? Do you embrace the basics of good business etiquette?
- How do you handle failure? Do you learn from the mistakes you make?

8

YOU, Improved

Reinventing Yourself
for Lifelong Success

"You have to leave the city of your comfort and go into the wilderness of your intuition. What you'll discover will be wonderful. What you'll discover is yourself."

—ALAN ALDA
Well-known American Actor and Personality

In this chapter you will begin to put together the ingredients that we talked about in the Science of Self-Improvement, which will enable you to feel better about yourself and walk with confidence. By following the guidelines that we have already discussed, and will now begin to apply, you will mold yourself into becoming a better job candidate, employee and a more confident person overall.

Adapting a positive and motivated attitude is one of the most important elements of becoming a stronger person. If you don't believe in yourself, how can you expect others to?

As Lewis Carroll, the author of *Alice's Adventures in Wonderland*, said: "If you don't know where you are going, any road will take you there."

You Are Free to Change

In going through this chapter, and as you go through life, you are going to take a look at what you're doing in life, and re-evaluate your choices. Everyone should periodically reevaluate where they are in life because if you don't like where you are, you can change. You are free to change at any time. You can change your job, your career path, your educational track, your location, your personal life . . . you can always make a change.

HAVE A PASSION

Remember the rule that *while sometimes you may fool other people, never fool yourself.* This means that, in reinventing yourself, you want to choose something that you not only believe you *can* do, but something that you *want* to do and are *truly excited about doing.*

For one thing, having a passion for something will make the job of convincing other people that you are excited about it, are energized and are an interesting person a lot easier. Not having to "fake it" puts you in a much better position because you can just act naturally.

Pursuing your passion is important because it's about you: *Your interests, your goals, your dreams.*

THIS BOOK IS ABOUT YOU

The SELF, Improved is not a book about acting out someone else's dreams or ambitions. It is about carefully evaluating the things that you want. Remember, you are following your priorities, not anyone else's. Therefore, the person you create and the image that you construct is, ultimately, *the person that you want to be.*

Pause for a moment to confirm that the plan you have laid out for yourself is really, truly, what you want. If it is not, now would be a very good time to go back to the charts and your priorities and readjust them so that you can move them in a different direction. *This is the last call. This is like the moment when the airline pilot tells you that if your destination isn't where the plane is going, you'd better get off and change planes before takeoff.* Because in the next few chapters, you are about to take off.

MAINTAIN YOUR NEW IMAGE AT ALL TIMES

Once you have learned the rules about appearance and image, emphasizing your strengths, communicating successfully, as well as learning how to handle criticism and remaining focused, *use these skills at all times.* Do this because it makes you look better in every setting, and with practice, your tools and techniques will become an unconscious behavior. They will be of benefit to you in almost every situation that you encounter.

Maintain your new polished image so that it becomes second nature.

Learning a New Language

Adopting a new image is similar to learning a new language in a new country. If you don't use the new language at all times, while on the job and at home, you won't make much improvement.

If you meet someone who's been in a new country for years but still doesn't speak the language very well, you can be almost positive that they speak in their native tongue at home. In contrast, people who speak their new language at home, not just at the workplace, can adapt and become familiar with their new culture very quickly.

CHANCE FAVORS ONLY THE PREPARED MIND

Another reason to maintain your image is that you never really know what new opportunities will present themselves, when they will present themselves, or where they will present themselves. You can meet people on planes, at business meetings, and in social settings. You never know who may become a potential business associate, a close personal friend, or simply someone that you can network with in the future.

Remember, first impressions are important. A lot of relationships just never happened and you may not even know that they *could have* happened because you were unprepared. Chance favors only the prepared mind.

You may have a friend who met somebody of importance in a social setting, leaving you to wonder why you weren't provided the same opportunity to meet that person. In fact, you might have had that very opportunity and just never knew about it. *You may not have been noticed because you didn't present the proper image.*

WEAR YOUR NEW SELF-IMAGE, PROUDLY

Remember that the image you're creating now is an image for your personal life and your professional life, so you want to wear that image just like clothing. The way you wear your hair, the way you dress, the way you carry yourself, the way you speak, it's all part of a package.

It's not an image that you've developed for somebody else. It's yours alone. It will help you obtain your objectives with someone else, *but it's for you and no one else.*

SET REALISTIC GOALS

Remember, in creating this image you want to set realistic goals.

If I set my goal in life to look like George Clooney I would be doomed to failure. Remember, we all have strengths and weaknesses—every single one of us. Choose the most dominant impression that you want to leave with people who see you. Then, *go one step further and take a look at what would also be easy to change.*

All kinds of people are successful in different areas, for different reasons. If Bill Gates had set his goal to "look like George Clooney," he, too, would have failed. Instead, he set a different goal and he was very successful at it. Today, he has become the richest man in the world. So when I say, "set realistic objectives," it doesn't mean set low objectives. It means, *set objectives that you can carry out.*

"There are three things extremely hard: steel, a diamond, and to know one's self."

—BENJAMIN FRANKLIN
Founding Father, Scientist, Author and Politician

An Appealing Package

Sometimes we look at someone and say, "What in the world does he or she do?"

Take Paris Hilton, for example. I keep trying to figure out what the phenomenon of Paris Hilton is all about. She is attractive, but other than that she is not well known for having accomplished anything of significance. But I can't dispute that she has become very successful. Obviously, she put together a package that appeals to the public.

There are many other examples of people we see in daily life who have done extraordinarily well and yet we can't really understand why.

HAVE A PLAN

Behind all successful people is one common denominator: *they all had a plan*. That is precisely what you need to succeed, too.

No matter what you do in life, you will have an edge if you have a plan. Structuring that plan is what this book is all about: combining your priorities with what you want for your image and then making them happen is your plan.

PRACTICE, PRACTICE, PRACTICE

"Practice does not make perfect. Only perfect practice makes perfect."

—VINCE LOMBARDI
World Famous American Football Coach
Member, Pro Football Hall of Fame

The look and the feel of the new you are like getting a new wardrobe; they are your image and they will define you.

Remember to stay focused on your objectives. Practice and wear your new attributes every day and all the time, like your favorite baseball cap or pair of jeans. This is your way of rehearsing. No performer will do well without a rehearsal.

Your job is to take this image and make it *you*. You do that by practice, practice, practice.

SELF-ASSESSMENT QUESTIONS

- Are you prepared for the expected? For the unexpected?
- Are you ready for new opportunities?
- Do you set goals that are achievable? Daily, weekly, in life?
- Have you reviewed your plan recently?

9

Your
CAREER,
Improved

Discovering the Pathway to Your Dreams

"Like my friend Warren Buffett, I feel particularly lucky
to do something every day that I love to do. He calls
it 'tap-dancing to work.'"

—BILL GATES
Businessman, Philanthropist and Founder of Microsoft

WHY CHANGE CAREERS?

*There are many reasons why people decide either to change careers or
to reenter the workplace.*

The decision to change careers sometimes takes place in a time
of anxiety, trepidation or emergency. During this period of
time people often assess what skills they have, what they want
to do and what image they want to project. The first chapters
of this book have already dealt with what kind of image you
want to project and how you can attain that image. This chapter
provides a more comprehensive summary of issues and

137

strategies that should be considered and acted upon in making career changes.

WHAT DO YOU WANT TO DO?

"Twenty years from now, you will be more disappointed by the things that you did not do than by the ones you did do."

—MARK TWAIN
Great American Author, Essayist and Humorist

The first thing you have to do when you decide to reenter the workplace or change your career is to determine what it is that you most want to do. Your chances of success will be a lot higher if you choose something for which you have a passion.

In some cases, you may be able to turn a passion or hobby into a career. Then, your job and your hobby can be one and the same. This is the best of both worlds, because you don't have to worry about the amount of time that you put into a job, *because it is something you already enjoy.*

CONSIDER YOUR MOTIVATION

Some people have a passion for helping others. Many areas of health care benefit from professionals like these because, for the most part, their workforce is motivated to take care of people rather than just make money.

There is nothing wrong with being motivated by money, but if that's your only motivation then you are less likely to be successful than somebody who gets satisfaction from doing the job well.

BE HONEST WITH YOURSELF

You should be honest about what you want to do and what you might have the talent to do. Also, if there are licenses or degrees required and you have to go back to school, you should take a look at the curriculum to know what kinds of studies are needed and to make sure you will be able to pass all subjects. If there is one class, such as chemistry, that you remember having difficulty with in high school, that's no reason to give up that profession. You must simply put that into your equation and make sure that you dedicate extra time to that course and, if necessary, get tutorial help.

BE HONEST WITH OTHERS

Considering Continuing Education

If you're going back to school and you think you might have a problem with one course, don't try to hide it from the people in the admissions process. Advisors at schools are there to help the students (Note: if a school doesn't take interest in providing that help, you don't want to go to that school anyway).

Good schools—and there are a lot of them out there—take interest in their students and want to help them make the right decisions. Be sure to be honest when you enter a program; it's the only way they can help you achieve your goal.

Be honest. This rule applies to job interviews and school admission interviews. If you can't get into a job or school when you are honest about yourself, don't bother. There are a lot of opportunities in the world, and life is too important to waste on people, organizations, or schools that won't accept you for who you are, especially when you are trying your best.

DON'T WASTE YOUR TIME

This principle applies to personal relationships as well. Anyone who will not accept you for who you are when you are trying your best is someone you don't need in your life. Just as there are many jobs, schools, and opportunities in the world, there are many potential partners as well. Don't waste your life and your time on someone who doesn't share your goals and aspirations.

DEVELOP AN ACTION PLAN

Once you've decided what it is you want to do and have ascertained that you can realistically attain that objective, your next job is to develop an action plan.

Your action plan might be getting a degree or going back to school. In some cases, if a profession that you want to go into is a licensed profession, it may be mandatory that you go to a specific type of school.

Time goes by quickly. Don't deprive yourself of what you really want to do in life because the program of study may take a year or two.

Look for schools or jobs that may offer financial aid or career training programs in order to get going in the direction of what you want.

It will be worth it. It is your major objective. There are some cases in which people have to work and bring in money immediately. If that is your situation, you might take a job that has some relationship to what you're interested in while going to school part-time. *Do all you can to get the education that you need to get into the profession that you really want.*

Don't accept second best.

MANY PATHS TO YOUR DREAM

Almost all people who are successful have one thing in common: *they set out to do something for which they have a passion.* It's rare to attain long-term, meaningful success in anything that's not of particular interest to you.

Never throw away your dreams and never let anyone talk you out of your dreams. It's never too late to seize your dreams. This is true even if your abilities are limited. If you think that realistically you simply cannot perform well at exactly what you always wanted to do in life, you can still enjoy a career that's closely related. For example, you may find that you can be accepted into a position that lets you work side-by-side or in partnership with people who have that job. You may find that this arrangement gives you satisfaction.

If it's clear that you can't obtain your ideal job right away, find out what your employer can do for you to help you get closer to your goal. In many cases, once you look into it, you'll find that you're *already* in an environment that will lead you to your dreams. Your employer may offer continuing education or training programs or have positions elsewhere in the company that will lead to the job you really want.

If the company is happy with you, but you're not happy with what you're doing, speak to the human resources department. They can guide you and inform you of other opportunities within the organization. They may also have special programs that include education, college tuition, or other benefits that will enable you to get where you want to go even with your present employer.

For example, if you really wanted to become a nurse and you can't get into nursing school, you might be able to get into the nursing system as an assistant and then take a pathway program provided by a hospital that over time will help you become a nurse.

The most important thing is to be in the type of environment that you want to be in for the goals that you really want to achieve in your professional career.

CHOOSE WHEN TO CHANGE: THE FIRST SIGNS

In order to get your action plan together, you often have to decide *when* it is time to make a change.

If you really, really are thinking about making a change . . . that's your first sign that it's probably time to move on.

You know better than anyone what's really on your mind, and if you are thinking about going through the rigorous steps to make a change in your life, it's probably because you know in your heart that you're not happy with what you're doing at the present time.

Many people wait too long to change. Don't be concerned or discouraged; this is human nature. Waiting to change happens in our jobs, in our investments, and in our relationships. The tendency to "throw good money after bad money" is part of being human.

Most individuals don't like to admit failure and many tend to stay too long at something they know is not working. But you don't have to make that mistake.

Your life is too short and time is too precious to waste it on something you don't really love to do.

Remember, it's never too late to start again. In fact, many people who were advanced in one career field have done very well with second careers. Often, this is because, in pursuing that second career, these individuals were forced to spend more time thinking about what they really wanted before making their decision.

ACCEPT CHANGE

Accepting change is not easy. Most people don't like change and the inconveniences that are involved. Usually, inconvenience is the main reason why people stay too long at something that's not right for them.

But change can also be fun, and a source of excitement. Once more, change can provide what the human spirit needs most in life: hope.

Hope that the future will be better than the past.

The hope that they can make the world a better place for future generations has kept many individuals going through hard times and has led to some of the greatest changes the world has seen.

For the Next Generation

Before Marie Curie's days as a brilliant scientist, she was faced with hardship that encouraged her to forge ahead and work towards a better future. As a child, Marie Curie's parents were ostracized for remaining loyal to their Polish heritage after their native city of Warsaw came under Russian rule. Because of their insistence on preserving Polish culture, Marie's parents were forced out of their jobs, leaving the family in financial turmoil. Before age 11, Marie endured the death of her sister from typhus followed soon after by her mother's losing battle with tuberculosis.

Despite her many hardships, Marie was determined to create a brighter future by completing her education at a University, and later went on to receive two Nobel Prizes. Along with her ultimate success, Marie remained true to her Polish identity, naming her first discovered chemical element polodium in honor of Poland, and then establishing a Radium Institute in her hometown of Warsaw, Poland.

CHANGE CAN BE FUN

Many of the changes that seem difficult, such as going back to school, can be fun if you view them in the right way. All of us have had experiences with certain courses and teachers that we didn't like. At the same time, we have also learned a great deal from teachers and courses that we loved. When you're older and considering a change of career or continuing your education, you have the advantage of taking the time and looking at things from a different perspective. Your knowledge of what you liked and didn't like can help you make the right decision about where to go with your future.

Make the most of it and enjoy the process of change. It is a part of life.

Change does not have to mean switching careers. It may involve a change in your place of employment or your duties within your current place of employment. Remember to utilize the help of your employer's human resources department if you wish to take on a new role in the company. They can help guide you to new positions and opportunities that may be available.

REVISIT YOUR LIST OF PRIORITIES

In deciding which path to take to make change a reality, go back and look at your priorities and your list of strengths and weaknesses. Doing so will help you determine how to project your strengths and minimize your weaknesses as you move forward.

Committing to Change

What does it mean to get around your weaknesses? In some cases, it can mean strengthening them.

A tennis coach decided that even though his student had solid groundstrokes, he believed that the student had to change his two-handed backhand to a one-handed stroke to be able to win at a professional level. From then on, the player practiced and competed with his new one-handed backhand. Along the way, he lost a lot of matches that he might have won had he used his old backhand. But he also strengthened his new backhand.

In the end, the player listened to his coach and demonstrated that he had great belief in improving himself—a belief so strong that he was willing to lose when he knew he could have won. A few years later, the player mastered that new backhand and went on to become the number one player in the world. His name: Pete Sampras.

You are in the process of improving yourself so you can be the best that you can be. You are looking at your weaknesses and deciding how you can overcome them.

Deciding to overcome your weaknesses doesn't mean you should force yourself to pursue something you are not good at. If you're bad at mathematics, you shouldn't choose to be an accountant and waste your time taking a lot of courses in math just to prove to others that you can do it. However, if mathematics is a course that you need to take in order to pursue something you really want, then take the time to get help and get past it.

In the above example of the tennis player, the coach's insistence to switch to a one-handed backhand did not prevent his player from competing with a competent forehand and backhand. Although his one-handed backhand may have cost him a few losses at first, the player was eventually able to perfect it, enabling him to become the top player in the world. Now fortunately, most of us do not need to work towards being "best in the world" at anything. If, however, there is certain knowledge required to succeed in the career that you want, and you are weak in these areas, you should take the time to learn and improve rather than just trying to hide from your weakness.

Keep Your Weaknesses in Perspective

Obviously, during something like a job interview, you're not going to emphasize your weaknesses. You're going to showcase your strengths. But don't be afraid of your weaknesses either; everybody has them. They are nothing to be embarrassed about.

Anyone who says they have no weaknesses has one big one: he is a liar.

DEVELOP A NEW PERSPECTIVE ON LIFE

It is said that *youth is wasted on the young*. One interpretation of this is, as we get older, things that were such a concern to us in our youth are no longer as important, so we can see what *really* matters with a greater degree of clarity.

If you are pursuing a different career when you are a little older, *experience* gives you a distinct advantage and helps you pursue your true career passion. That is the benefit of having a different perspective on life, one based on having been around for a while. Excited and focused as we all were about getting into the right college, the right company or the "in" group, we realize that people from all walks of life become successful, not only because of the colleges they attended or groups that they belong to, but also because of their own abilities and passions. This understanding is a distinct advantage you gain with age and experience. Use it to your benefit.

When you do present yourself to others in your journey to reinvent yourself, make sure that you position yourself as the right person for the job or for the promotion. Use the tools we talked about in previous chapters.

ASCERTAIN IF YOU WILL FIT IN

If you're going to interview with a company, learn something about that company. Learn what they are like and what they do. Try to fit in. Once you are part of a company and you want to advance, make sure it is in a place where you feel comfortable and recognized. If you're going into a school for an admissions interview, read the mission statement of the school, understand what the school is about, and try to place yourself within the context of that school. If you honestly can't see yourself fitting in with the profile of the school, find another one.

Remember: interviews for careers, new assignments, or for schools are a two-way street. It's not just about whether they want you, it's also about whether or not you want *them*.

This is your life. You only have one and this is your chance to make the most of it.

REEVALUATE YOUR LIFE CHOICES

Wise people in the stock market always say that if you wouldn't buy a stock at the level it is at now, then sell it. This is true about where you are in life as well.

If you don't like where you are in life now, change it.

Whether it's your job, your profession, your education or your personal life, you can always make a change. Everyone should make it a habit to periodically reevaluate where they are in life. The biggest mistake that people make is they make one mistake and they go through with that mistake for the rest of their lives.

If nothing else, this book will teach you that you have many options and that you can always make a change, no matter where you are in your life, if you don't think it's right for you.

Don't be afraid of looking at your life honestly. If you think that doing so is going to be disruptive, then you know in your heart that you are not happy with where you are. You should be making a change. It is better to know how you feel honestly, than to live a life that isn't satisfying to you.

The SELF, Improved is your guide to help you make those changes as easily as possible.

SELF-ASSESSMENT QUESTIONS

- Do you like where you are in your life or do you have thoughts about making a change?
- Do you know what you want to change about your life? Can you be concrete about it?
- What is your motivation for your career choice? Money? Passion? Security? Self-fulfillment?
- How do you deal with change? Do you embrace it? Fear it? Avoid it?

SECOND
SELF-ASSESSMENTS

CHART IV:
WHAT DO YOU WANT?
WHERE DO YOU WANT TO GO?

Review the list of professions on the following page. Are you currently working in the field you want to be in? If so, that is great! Rank it #1.

But if you are having thoughts of changing careers or jobs, remember . . . it is never too late to change. So start by ranking, one to three, the professions you are most interested in pursuing (#1 = most interested, #2 next most interested, etc.).

Write in any that may not be listed on the chart . . . this is just a guide.

FIELD	PROFESSION	RANK (1st, 2nd, 3rd)
ARTS & SCIENCES	MEDICAL	
	RESEARCH	
	TEACHING	
	ACADEMICS	
	ENGINEERING	
	INTERNET TECHNOLOGY	
	BIOTECH	
FASHION/CREATIVE ARTS	DESIGNER/CREATOR	
	PERFORMER/MUSICIAN/ACTOR	
	DIRECTOR	
	WRITER/COMPOSER	
	MODEL	
	ARTIST	
SPORTS/ATHLETIC	COACH/TRAINER	
	ATHLETE	
	MANAGER	
FINANCE/BUSINESS	ENTREPRENEUR/ HAVE YOUR OWN BUSINESS	
	BANKING/FINANCIAL SERVICES	
	ADMINISTRATION/CLERICAL	
	ACCOUNTANT	
	MANUFACTURING	
	INVESTMENTS	
	PERSONNEL	
	PURCHASING	
	INSURANCE	
	MEDIA/JOURNALISM	
	TRANSPORTATION	
MARKETING/SALES	PRODUCT MANAGEMENT	
	SALES MANAGER	
	SALES REP	
	RETAIL	
	ADVERTISING	
	PUBLIC RELATIONS	
	TRAINING	
HEALTH CARE	PRACTITIONER/PROVIDER	
	TEACHER	
	ADMINISTRATOR	
	PHARMACEUTICAL	
SERVICE INDUSTRY	HOSPITALITY	
	CONSULTING	
	FOOD SERVICE/RESTAURANT	
	GOVERNMENT	
	REAL ESTATE	
	LEGAL	
	LAW ENFORCEMENT/SECURITY	
GENERAL LABOR	FACTORY	
	CONSTRUCTION	
	MAINTENANCE/REPAIR	
OTHER		

CHART V:
PERSONAL ASSESSMENT
FOR YOUR PROFESSION

On a scale of 1 to 10, in your opinion, how important are these traits for the professions you wish to be in?

(1 = not at all important and 10 = the most important.)

Copy the three professions you just selected onto the following chart and now evaluate the Attribute list thinking about these specific career paths. Remember, you can give the same rating to more than one trait.

ATTRIBUTES/TRAITS	HOW IMPORTANT ARE THESE TRAITS IN (fill in your #1 Profession) Rate each on a scale of 1 to 10	HOW IMPORTANT ARE THESE TRAITS IN (fill in your #2 Profession) Rate each on a scale of 1 to 10	HOW IMPORTANT ARE THESE TRAITS IN (fill in your #3 Profession) Rate each on a scale of 1 to 10
Overall Appearance			
Dress Well/Nice Clothing			
Healthy Weight			
Hair			
Grooming			
Facial Appearance—Skin/Makeup			
Overall Physical Carriage			
Posture			
Body Language			
Open/Confident/Poised			
Strong/Vibrant/Energetic			
Overall Communication Skills			
Speech			
Writing			
Good Listener			
Clarity			
Speaking in Public			
Overall Intelligence and Aptitude			
Educated			
Experienced			
Street Smart			
Talented			
Well-Versed in Current Affairs			
Good with Numbers and Math			
Read and Write Well			
Overall Personality			
Confident			
Ambitious/Motivated			
Serious/Reliable			
Friendly/Happy			
Caring/Considerate/Tolerant			
Patient			
Relate Well to Others			
Cool Under Pressure or Stress			
Overall Professional Skills			
Leadership			
Organized			
Multi-Tasker/Time Management			
Preparedness			
Motivator			
Computer Ability			
Clear Thinker			
Overall Etiquette			
Personal Manners			
Business Manners			
Overall Health			
Physically Fit			
Eat Well			
Sleep Well			
Strong/Vibrant/Energetic			

10

Your
NETWORKING SKILLS,
Improved
Connecting for Success

"More business decisions occur over lunch and dinner
than at any other time, yet no MBA courses are given
on the subject."

—PETER DRUCKER,
World Renowned Author and Economist
The Future of Industrial Man and
Concept of the Corporation

Whether you're looking for a job or expanding the
reach of your present job, networking is an extremely
important tool. Over 80 percent of the jobs today are not
advertised, and that percentage increases for executive level
positions.

*One of the ways that people often find jobs is by talking to other people
socially. Your search can be facilitated by associating with the right
people.*

Networking is *not* about using other people. Rather, networking should benefit both parties involved. Remember, employers or potential employers are just as eager to find the right person for a job as the person seeking a job. Finding the right person is important for an employer. Always keep in mind that the relationship between an employer and employee is also a two-way street.

WHAT NETWORKING IS NOT

Some people try to use friends or relatives to get to a higher position than they really deserve. This never works out. It just becomes a waste of everybody's time and an embarrassment to the person who gave you the opportunity. Furthermore, it is likely that no one is going to give you a second opportunity if you get a reputation for using and taking advantage of others.

If you view networking as a means to get someplace that you don't belong simply because you know somebody, you're making a big mistake. People can only go to the level they have prepared for and where they can perform well, if they are ready. They cannot leapfrog and take a job that they are not qualified for, just by knowing somebody and having an inside track. This is important to realize, because so many people believe that other people who have gotten their jobs through networking got the job just because they met the right person. This leads people to assume that, if they were given the same opportunity and "knew" someone, that they would get the job easily.

Nothing could be further from the truth.

Occasionally, someone may give a person a job because he or she is a friend, or family. That's called *nepotism*, and the person could actually lose his job for doing that. It is not part of the ethical standards by which companies are run. If an employer happens to know somebody who could really do the job, that may not be considered nepotism, as long as the person is genuinely qualified. If, however, the person lacks the qualifications, it's dangerous for the employer to hire that person—more likely than not, he won't be able to hold onto the job.

Making Introductions

In my businesses I've come across people who have a great deal of power. Some acquaintances who are aware of this come to me and say, "Can't you introduce my son or daughter to one of these people?"

I always reply with the same question, "What does your son or daughter have to offer this person?" It's amazing how many people don't have an answer to that very simple question!

If they don't have an answer to that, nothing will happen for their son or daughter. Why? Because the person who's important is already besieged by people who are looking for jobs. They will only give their time to people who they know can truly help them.

NETWORKING CASTS A WIDE NET

So, what is networking?

According to Merriam-Webster, one definition is the following: "the exchange of information and services among individuals, groups and institutions; specifically: the cultivation of productive relationships for employment or business."

Here is another definition:

Networking is the conscious participation in social and professional events for the sole purpose of expanding your opportunities for success.

Networking at parties, social events, political and industry events is essential to allow you to reach out and, in some cases, find out about job openings. Networking provides you with the ability to cast a much larger net, and meet a larger group of people than you would normally encounter in your regular job.

This may give you an opportunity to learn about other companies and even let you know who the decision makers are at those firms.

NETWORKING PROVIDES PERSPECTIVE

Networking also has psychological benefits. It's important for you to remember that the problems that come up in your company or in your work situation are not unique or limited to your situation. People with similar jobs in similar industries tend to have similar problems. Meeting other people who share the same problems helps reduce your sense of anxiety and isolation.

It also lets you know that there are other individuals who are looking for jobs, so *the fact that you're looking for a job doesn't mean that you are a failure.*

YOUR NETWORKING TOOLS

The skills of networking are very much like the other skills presented in *The SELF, Improved*. As you learned, the *good news* about networking is that it is now one of the primary tools through which corporations and businesses find new employees. However, for some of us, meeting new people may be stressful and anxiety-producing. Negative messages can present themselves, such as, "I'm not good enough, smart enough, attractive enough," etc.

Using what you've learned in *The SELF, Improved*, refocus your mind on the following:

> I am prepared. I look my best. I know what I need to do and say and how to do it. I know my objectives and goals and I am excited about this event because it will take me one step closer to achieving them.

Jeffrey Meshel, author of *One Phone Call Away: Secrets of a Master Networker*, provides this wisdom:

- *What you know facilitates who you know. What you know dictates how lucky you become.*
- *Make the person you are speaking with feel like he or she is the most important person you know (relatively speaking, of course).*
- *Good judgment comes from experience. Experience comes from bad judgment.*

BE HONEST IN NETWORKING

The main thing to remember in networking is: *don't try to fool anyone or overstate your position.* You may lose out on a very valuable opportunity if you start out by saying you're something that you're not.

For example, somebody might say they are making a higher salary than they really are—and then find out that there's really a perfect job available at a lower salary. Now this person may not ever be considered for the job because he pretended to make more than he really does, and the employer won't think to offer it to him. Or, somebody could say he's making a higher salary, and, when he applies for a job and the human resources department asks to see his W-2 forms, he has to hand them over and he gets caught in his lie. Now the opportunity is lost, since given the choice between being a liar or providing the forms, people tend to avoid getting caught and back out.

BE COMFORTABLE

In networking, be yourself, be comfortable and present yourself in a way that is truthful. When you have the opportunity to network and you meet with somebody who really can help you, make sure that what you have to deliver is *real*.

So the most important thing in networking is to be comfortable and to present yourself the way you want to present yourself. *Be truthful.*

IDENTIFY WHAT YOU CAN DELIVER

When you do meet somebody who you think could be important to you, try to quickly ascertain what it is that you have to offer—*and let them know it*. This rule applies even if that person isn't hiring. Why? If someone is highly influential and successful and they meet an individual who encompasses certain skills or attributes that they need, they're going to be interested in that individual whether or not they have a position open at the moment.

So be ready to tell the person as quickly and as clearly as possible, *what it is that you do* and *why you can be of value*. Describe what you have to offer in the same way as you would in a job interview. The only difference is that at a networking event the mood is generally less formal and more pleasant, but the time parameter with any one person will probably be shorter.

A note on interacting with "Important People": Nobody likes it when someone is wasting their time, least of all important people. When individuals meet an important person, they often make the mistake of asking that person to do something for them. It's really the other way around!

Have Something Special to Offer

For 25 years I have been a partner in many ventures, often with some of the largest companies in the world. A lot of people who know this about me ask if they can meet the top officers of a company. Often, they want to secure an interview at the company, as well.

The problem with executives at very large companies is that they meet lots of applicants on a consistent basis and unless you have something very special to offer, they're not really going to be interested. They may listen out of politeness, but then they'll have their human resources departments get rid of you—and you'll never know what happened.

If you have too high an expectation of yourself and you lack the experience, don't expect to derive something from a networking or a social situation that you could not otherwise derive from a professional relationship based on your skill set. That's the key.

DO YOUR RESEARCH

The same research that goes into learning about a company before you go on a job interview should also be done before attending a networking event. It may give you a certain advantage, but don't overestimate its value.

Additionally, pay the same attention to clothing, appearance, and other details of presenting yourself when networking. Use what you've learned in the other chapters about job interviews as guidelines. Meeting new people may give you a slight edge and an opportunity to find out about jobs before they are posted and before you have more competition.

FOLLOW-THROUGH

After you meet somebody, take the time to follow through. Athletes know that follow-through is part of the game; people without follow-through don't do well in sports. They also don't do well in business or business situations.

Once you make contact, take the time to thank the person for their time, and follow up the next day or the same week with an e-mail, phone call, or letter. If the person did something for you or gave you some information, send them a handwritten note or a small, thoughtful gift. What's important here is to be and act appreciative of their time.

Show them that you acknowledge what they did for you. *This is the first sign in showing appreciation for the networking system.*

The SELF, Improved is preparing you for success.

SELF-ASSESSMENT QUESTIONS

- Do you recognize the role of the various people in your life?
- Do you network and expand your contacts?
- Are you comfortable meeting new people? Meeting important people?

11

Your
TIME and MONEY,
Improved
Managing Your Most Important Assets

"But money is only a tool. It will take you wherever you wish, but it will not replace you as the driver."

—AYN RAND
Philosopher, Writer and Founder of Objectivism
Altas Shrugged

O ne of the most important skills in the workplace or in your personal life is going to be your ability to manage your time and your money. These are important in the context of self-improvement and self-esteem. We live in a society that judges people by the amount of money they make and the amount of money that their departments or companies generate. While this may not be your objective in and of itself, *it is a scorecard by which people measure your success.*

This chapter will discuss how you can plan deadlines, prioritize your work, handle multitasking, manage your credit and budget, and talk about saving money and investing.

MONEY AND SELF-ESTEEM

Before getting into the specifics of money management, you must first understand that issues of self-esteem go hand-in-hand with your success in handling money and the amount of money that you make. This is very important to keep in mind.

Almost everyone knows the example of Mother Teresa. Although Mother Teresa did, in fact, earn money for her charities, she is generally known for her selfless work on behalf of others. Society appreciates her for this. In most cases, however, society determines whether people are important by how much money they make. Because of this, many people want to make a lot of money.

But they make a mistake when they think that somehow this money will bring them happiness.

Wealthy people know that money does not bring happiness.

I have had a career that has had many ups and downs. It has given me the chance to look at my life and ask myself, was I any happier during the periods of time when I had the most money compared to times when I had less money?

The truth is, for me, *there was no correlation.*

I never, however, lacked self-worth. So remember that, if your self-worth is tied to what other people think of you, then you may in fact end up living in a way that is closely linked to what society generally thinks: that wealthy people are most important.

Undeserved Admiration

It's always amazing to me that notorious financial figures, such as Marc Rich, are often admired, even though the way they made money was not particularly admirable.

THE KENNEDY PARADOX

The Kennedys are a great example of how money can elevate someone's status in the eyes of society—no matter how the money was earned. Many don't know that Joe Kennedy made his money in bootlegging (smuggling illegal liquor) during Prohibition and he was in many ways not that much different from Al Capone. Yet, his family is regarded as American royalty and the money he obtained through his bootlegging operations helped build an American dynasty which people have respected on all levels.

When Jacqueline Kennedy married Aristotle Onassis, there was a tremendous outcry that the former First Lady of the United States had married somebody for money. But as the years passed, people forgot and revered Jackie and the decision she made to ensure financial security for herself and her children.

Money is not going to make you happy necessarily, nor is it a worthy objective in and of itself. *But it is a status symbol, so to disregard it as such would be a mistake.*

MAKING MISTAKES IS HUMAN

People who trade in the stock market and invest their money always blame themselves when they make a bad investment. They often don't sell their bad investments early enough—they try to wait for them to rebound. They act in this way because they don't want to face the situation honestly. This leads to big mistakes.

Making a mistake is human, so you're going to make a lot of mistakes; we all do. Fixing those mistakes is a challenge. It's what makes life worth living.

KNOWING THE ENDING AHEAD OF TIME IS BORING

During my life I have spent a lot of time at the racetrack. Later on in life I learned that the reason why gambling is so exciting is not because you think that you're going to win, but because the chance of losing provides just as much excitement as the chance of winning.

If you were to go to the racetrack every single day and you knew that you would win every single race, you might like keeping the money, but you'd be bored out of your mind. What would be the point of watching the race? You would already know the end.

It's the same way in life: for many, without the excitement of winning and losing, life becomes boring.

The Greatest Movies

Think of life like going to the movies. Who would want to go to a movie that told the story of a person who made a lot of money and was very successful, made more money, lived a perfect life, and then died? That's not a good plot for a movie.

People want to see a movie where somebody has some success, gains a fortune, loses it—and then makes a comeback. Comeback movies are always interesting. This is because people like to see someone come back from failure to be successful again.

We all know that a lot of celebrities take drugs and alcohol and end up with terrible problems. We wonder why people who are so successful end up in rehabilitation clinics. The answer is simple: *it is because, in many cases, when people are successful and don't have to face any more risks in life, the element of excitement is gone from their existence.*

So some people try to find a substitute for the element of risk through the abuse of substances and stimulants.

Not a Straight Road

Being successful is usually not a straight road in one direction or a one-way street. To be really successful in this world I think you have to make it, have a major setback, experience the bitter taste of failure—and then come back and make it again.

If you take a really good look at people who are retired, you will see a lot of very unhappy people. Individuals spend their whole lives waiting to retire to their "place in the sun" and, before they get there, think, "this is going to be paradise." More often than not, it ends up not being paradise at all. Instead, there is nothing for them to do.

Money, luxury, and relaxation do *not* automatically bring happiness.

MONEY IS A TOOL

The SELF, Improved is not going to tell you to get rid of all your worldly possessions and not make any money. Rather, *The SELF, Improved* is about giving you the tools that you need to go out in society *and make as much money as you possibly can to help you meet your goals, given your abilities.*

The purpose of this explanation is to tell you that even with these tools and even with success (and that's what *The SELF, Improved* is about—success through self-improvement), happiness is not directly related to money. It may be related to your self-worth, but success and happiness are very complicated. To be sure, it is better to have more money than less, but there are a lot of things that are more important than just making money.

As Dr. Frederic Flach, author of *Resilience*, wrote:

> How much money you personally need is how much money you need to do and accomplish the things you want to accomplish. Money is a wonderful thing. You can do all sorts of things with money. You can buy time with money. You can go out and spend money on your education. You can go out and spend money on taking

care of your physical health. You can spend money on stimulating your mind and your imagination.

For the purposes of this book, how to make money and making the most out of money are the tools that I will try to give you. It's up to you, though, to find true happiness.

LEARN FROM YOUR MONEY MISTAKES

What you do with your money and whether or not it brings you happiness is not the subject of this book. It is important, however, that you have the right perspective when it comes to managing and investing your money. The key is to look at money somewhat dispassionately and understand that you might make some mistakes, but know that everybody makes mistakes. Your mistakes should be a guidepost for your future.

We are often led to our successes by our failures.

If we were all good at everything then we wouldn't be able to find out which path to take. If you're bad at writing, don't become a journalist. If you've got a poor voice, don't become a singer. Learning what our limitations are will ultimately help us make the right choices and guide our lives by focusing on our strengths.

That is what the assessment charts are all about.

The charts that you filled in tell you what's important to you and then correlate your abilities to the traits that you value so you can make the right choices in life.

YOUR LIFE, YOUR CHOICES

There are choices that only *you* can make, which is why your charts are individualized. This book doesn't give you a pre-determined filled out chart, and I don't want you to copy someone else's chart.

You shouldn't do what your parents want for you, or try to project what someone else wants for you. In order for you to be successful and get what you truly want, these choices have to be *your* choices. It doesn't mean, however, that you're going to accomplish everything you want.

Weigh the Amount of Risk You Want to Take

The amount of risk that you take is often going to be related to your personal wish to make it big.

It's not important to everyone to lead an adventuresome life. Determining how much excitement you want is part of the introspection that you must undertake. You have to take a look at yourself and when you're making your choices, ask, "Is it more important to me that I have a stable life, or an exciting life?"

UNFORESEEN CIRCUMSTANCES

Not only do you need to work within the limits of your own abilities, but there is also the element of chance. There are always unforeseen circumstances in life.

You Can't Know It All

I had a friend who was the black sheep of his very rich family. He decided he was going to make a lot of money by taking one topic and learning more about it than anyone in the world. The topic he chose was cocoa futures (a sophisticated financial investment).

This man studied everything there was to know about cocoa futures, particularly in Africa. He analyzed everything about this crop—weather conditions, demand and supply side economics, and more—in short, everything that he could possibly know about growing and selling cocoa. He then invested a tremendous amount of money, most of which was given to him by his family, in cocoa futures.

Ultimately, he was wiped out because there was an elephant stampede in Africa that destroyed the cocoa fields. An elephant stampede is something that no one in the world could ever have imagined would have had an effect on cocoa futures.

You simply can't predict every circumstance.

So whatever it is that you think that you can do, don't try to control everything in your environment. Forget it, since there are always unforeseen circumstances. Don't hold yourself responsible for things that you couldn't see or can't control.

Aristotle, the great philosopher, once wrote that *"praise and blame attach to voluntary actions."* You can't blame yourself for things that are outside of your control.

Furthermore, don't spend too much time looking backward. The purpose of looking backward is to learn and educate yourself. Education can be painful, but if used properly, education is your most valuable tool in leading you to a successful future.

START SOMEWHERE

As with all things in life that require work, you have to start somewhere. Archimedes, the great inventor and mathematician, said, *"Give me a lever long enough and a fulcrum on which to place it, and I shall move the world."*

What did he mean? He meant that it is very important that you have a place to stand. You must know what matters to you. If you don't, and you don't have a place to stand, then you can get pushed around following other people's advice or objectives. You have to be grounded.

How do you get a place to stand? You do it by setting objectives, priorities and deadlines. If you don't have deadlines then the objectives and the priorities may be impacted by your life, but things will never be completed.

Why? There's always a reason for not doing something.

SET A DEADLINE

A lot of people say they would have done something like write a book or start a business *if they had only had the time*. The truth is that most people don't get things done because they don't set personal deadlines.

Many of us are given professional deadlines on a regular basis. These deadlines are ones we understand and adhere to. You should set personal deadlines and adhere to them, as well. Having personal deadlines for anything you want to accomplish is vital, yet most people don't set them. Don't make this mistake.

When you set your objectives and base them on your priorities, you should also set a *reasonable* deadline.

Deadlines have to be realistic or you're going to miss them. If you miss your deadlines then you might as well not have them. This is very much like dieting.

Avoid Frustration

Everybody will tell you that if you want to lose weight and go on a diet, set realistic objectives. If you say you want to lose 25 pounds a week, it's not going to happen. You will become frustrated and end up not dieting.

The same thing is true for deadlines. If they're realistic and you can meet your deadlines, then you will be way ahead of the game.

So, deadlines are important in everything that you do. Even when accomplishing your goals on appearance in the first chapters, you should set yourself a timeline which has deadlines. If you keep changing your *timelines* and don't establish an absolute *deadline*, there will always be a reason to put something off.

Stick To It No Matter What

Athletes who train for events know the importance of deadlines, goals, and discipline very well. A formal exercise schedule becomes almost like a religious event, and without fail an athlete must follow it.

You must behave in a similar way. There is always a party, there is always a friend asking you out to dinner—there is always something that you would rather do than the tasks that make up your deadlines, but if you don't make certain things absolute priorities they just won't happen.

ORGANIZE YOUR TIME AT THE OFFICE

"Determine never to be idle. No person will have occasion to complain of the want of time who never loses any. It is wonderful how much can be done if we are always doing."

—THOMAS JEFFERSON
Founding Father and
Third President of the United States

You have to organize your work-related activities.

In *5 Steps to Professional Presence: How to Project Confidence, Competence, and Credibility at Work*, authors Susan Bixler and Lisa Scherrer Dugan provide an example of an easy, effective way to prevent others from wasting your time in the office, by using body language. When someone stops by your office and interrupts you with conversation, Bixler suggests,

> Use a straightforward solution—stand up. If you are seated and busy and someone walks into your work-space and you don't want interruption, stand up and stay standing...They will generally get the point and leave.

A method like this has the added benefit, points out Bixler, of being subtle enough that, most likely, it will not offend the other person.

Most people who really want to get ahead have to do some preparation that's related to their work.

Time management is a very important factor in anyone's life. Whether in family, business, hobbies or new activities, time allocation determines success.

A turning point in my life occurred when, many years ago, I took a good, honest look at how I was spending my time. I went back over business expenses and diaries and closely examined what percentages of my meetings were successful. It was a dismal experience. Less than 5 percent of what I was doing accounted for generating all my future business.

The big question was, could I have known which 95 percent of my time I was wasting, as I was wasting it?

The answer is "yes," we all pretty much know when we are wasting our time, but some of the projects seem like fun or give us personal satisfaction (which may not be a waste of time, but may not help out much in our future).

We all have to get rid of as much "noise" as possible so we can go directly to our objectives.

KNOW WHAT'S GOING ON

Even people who work 9 to 5 and want to keep that 9 to 5 schedule will not get ahead unless they do more and follow what is happening in the world that relates to their job activities. This knowledge should be combined with what they know about where they work.

By knowing what's going on at your level of work, whatever level that is, and integrating it with what's happening in the world, you not only improve your performance on your job, but you also become a standout in your organization.

So if you're in a consumer products industry, and you realize from a newspaper article that the demographics for your product are changing, don't just say, "Well, that's not my business, I am not a manager. I'm not the president of the company."

Take the initiative to bring it to the attention of your boss. Take the time and effort to send your input from your level up the proper channels of communication. Your awareness at *your* level can sometimes help people at a *higher* level find solutions that they may not know about, since they don't work on the ground floor of their organizations. You can provide them with perspective.

Believe me, people who express concerns will be handsomely rewarded by most management. Management wants people who are loyal, productive, and able to think out-of-the-box and share insights from where they stand with different levels of management.

From the Battlefield

The viewpoint of a soldier on the battlefield may be very important to a general sitting at the Pentagon or command center. Everybody who uses a certain type of rifle may know the shortcomings of that rifle, but unless it's communicated to the purchasing people at the Department of Defense, soldiers will keep getting defective rifles. The person who makes the purchases doesn't necessarily have to use that product on the battlefield.

This is an example of the importance of communicating what's taking place "on the ground" with the people who are trying to control things from far away.

So never take anything for granted. *Your insights are valuable.* If people are doing their jobs properly, what they do is valuable not only for the work itself, but for the insights that they can provide to others.

BEWARE OF UNREASONABLE EXPECTATIONS

You have to organize your work-related activities so as not to take on too much or to provide too little service. In the organizational process you may find that you have too much work and can't do the job properly. Bring that to the attention of your superiors as quickly as possible, because it's neither in their interest nor yours to set yourself up with unreasonable expectations.

Showing that you've organized your work-related activities not only helps your performance but also allows you to have a clearer picture and makes your work easier to deal with.

PACE YOURSELF

The other thing you have to do in any kind of job or even in your personal life is to pace yourself and make sure that you get the job done.

People who are energetic and don't pace themselves always run into problems. If you're in a marathon, don't try to go out there and be a sprinter and run the best time ever—you know that you're not going to be able to maintain that pace throughout the entire race. You run the risk of not finishing at all. This happens all too often—people who want to prove themselves start off at an energetic pace that's unrealistic to maintain over a period of time.

When that happens, they show that they've created unreasonable expectations and people perceive them as faltering.

You should plan your day or week in advance and pace yourself so that you don't set up unrealistic expectations on the part of others. When problems come up you should deal with them squarely and with some degree of dispassion. Don't think you are a terrible person because you made a mistake or because something unexpected comes along.

Don't Show Your Hand

I had a partner who made sure that the day a bill came in he would pay it. He was so fastidious about this that if somebody sent him a bill it would be paid in one or two days. Another person who was not as fastidious took one or two weeks to pay a similar bill.

What happens in this case? If the bill is not due and it's always paid immediately, then if anything does happen to the person (such as someone else not paying him on time), everyone knows immediately that he's in trouble. When the person who pays two or three weeks out is late, nobody knows if he is in trouble immediately because they say, "Oh, they always pay eventually."

So sometimes it's not an advantage to show your hand and do everything so quickly so that it becomes expected of you. This clearly does not mean that you should make late payments (because your credit scores will be lowered and that's really bad in today's economy), but it does mean that you shouldn't be so fanatical about getting everything done and off your plate that you create an unrealistic pace for yourself. Then, when something unforeseen comes up, you've established a precedent that can't always be maintained and you will let others down.

PROBLEM SOLVING

Problem solving is one of my favorite fields. As an inventor, I look at all problems as potential patents. Problems and problem solving are ways for you to see things that are probably not unique to you but are experienced by a lot of people. If you can find a great solution to a problem, assume that that solution will be of value to others.

Hence the expression, "Necessity is the mother of invention."

From Problem to Invention

I had a cat many years ago that insisted on using all my plants as a litter box. I happened to have been doing a project in the "inflatables" business at the time. I decided to use a clear inflatable to create a terrarium around my plants so that my cat couldn't get to the soil to use my plants as a litter box. I realized after I had constructed this product that the plants were doing exceptionally well inside this clear terrarium. Remember the expression from Louis Pasteur that "chance favors only the prepared mind."

I was able to recognize that the plants were growing faster and saw that there was something different about these inflatable coverings that I had made because of a problem I was having with my cat. It turned out that when you blow into an inflatable object, you create positive air pressure.

Inadvertently, I had created the first hyperbaric chamber for plants. I ended up getting patents on it, and created a multi-million dollar business. It also created a system by which seedlings and all plants could be grown at greater speeds, all because my cat kept using my plants as a litter box.

So problems not only give way to solutions, but those solutions can provide new products and new solutions if you keep an open mind and don't view every problem as a bad thing. Over the years, I've grown to love problems. Whereas other people dislike the "problems of living," I've taken them and turned them into hundreds of consumer products that have generated tremendous amounts of money in many different areas.

When you have a problem to solve, the most important thing is to identify specifically what the real problem is, and then go to your home base of knowledge and work out the solution.

Unlearning Limits

In some ways, the Internet and Google searches—things that many of the younger generations are growing up with—have hurt us because they tell us what's been done. We've been trained from an early age to believe that everything we think of has already been done and that there's nothing new left to do. That's a lot of garbage.

Every young child, before he or she goes into the conventional school system, has imagination and ways of solving problems. Many of these spontaneous solutions to problems are drilled out of people as their schooling progresses. Much of the imagination of the human mind is lost because everybody has a way of doing something that they've been taught.

DON'T REPEAT
WHAT'S ALREADY BEEN SAID

Problem solving can be one of your biggest assets. But don't confuse problem solving with providing an easy answer. If, in the workplace, you simply repeat what everybody else has been doing, it limits your ability to advance. If your managers or superiors already know what you present to them and you are merely repeating yourself, this shows that you have limited ability and you miss a chance to use your imagination and knowledge.

MASTERING MULTITASKING

Multitasking is something that everybody talks about and most people don't do particularly well.

In many jobs people are required to multitask; that is, they are asked to do more than one thing at the same time. If you follow the first part of the chapter and organize your objectives, priorities and deadlines, and you organize your work-related activities, then you will be able to successfully handle multitasking.

Avoid "Jumping"

If you don't have an organized structure to help you accomplish multiple tasks, more often than not you will start one project only to be interrupted by another. Then, you will have to complete the second one before returning to the first project. Jumping back and forth like this is distracting for most people. Therefore, most "multitaskers" end up using their time inefficiently, and, even worse, end up producing work of poorer and poorer quality with each successive task.

Advice from Experts

HOW TO MULTITASK

Prioritize. If you want to multitask, you need to know what is most important. For example, spending hours filing old reports probably isn't nearly as important as that Excel spreadsheet your boss asked you to complete by the end of the workday.

Make a schedule. Humans, as the saying goes, are creatures of habit. If you have something that has to be done every day, set aside the same amount of time every day to do it. If you have one hour and three tasks to finish, give yourself twenty minutes per task. If one task is more important than another (for instance, creating your boss's Excel spreadsheet as opposed to filing old reports), designate thirty minutes for the higher priority task and fifteen minutes for the others. You can split up the time for your tasks any way you like, but the idea is to set limits for yourself so you can accomplish your goals.

Focus on one task. Your brain is designed to process one task at a time. The most effective way to multitask is to complete, or get as far as you can on, the highest priority task and then immediately move on to the next task.

Remember what still needs to be done. In most jobs you will be required to multitask. In your personal life, you're usually required to multitask, juggling household tasks with family obligations and even occasionally bringing work home.

ANTICIPATE THE UNEXPECTED

Again, the solution is to anticipate the unexpected and organize your schedule so that these interruptions are planned for and you have a way of working them into your comprehensive schedule.

We all have experiences where everything cannot be planned. Somebody dies and you and your family have to take time off at a critical time. You can't have a calendar or a schedule that says, "I can't be interrupted by a death in the family."

There are times that your schedule is going to be disrupted, but as soon as it is, you have to go back to your calendar, put in time for the extraneous event and then go back to your organized plan. You can't throw away your organization, your objectives, your priorities and your deadlines just because something unexpected happened.

CREDIT AND MONEY MANAGEMENT

During our professional and personal lives, we all have to deal with credit. Monetary credit, that is.

We live in a credit society. When we first get credit, there is a temptation to overspend. The events of 2008 and 2009 will go down in history as the time in which our capitalistic system expended so much credit, and put so much pressure on people to use this credit, that virtually all of our great institutions collapsed. This has created a "sea change" in how people view credit, and has changed our perspective on credit for the future.

Credit can be a good thing to have and use. Positive uses of credit include using it to build a company that will generate revenue in the future, using it in times of emergency, or using it as part of a managed business plan. It is never a good idea to use credit frivolously.

Credit gives people the illusion that they have more money than they really do. That's one of the reasons why financial institutions provide easy credit and raise credit limits: to encourage people to spend. These companies know that in the end, they will profit from high interest rates because people will spend more than they have and fail to pay their credit cards off on time.

Casinos love giving credit because they know you're going to take it. They want you to gamble with that money and lose. Then they know they're going to earn a lot of interest as you slowly pay it back. *Remember, it's always easier to spend money than it is to pay it back.*

SKILLS FOR MANAGING CREDIT

Shop around. Examine offers from various banks and card companies for criteria including rates, benefits and affordability.

Pay off the balance. When you pay off your monthly balance on time, you won't accrue any interest or additional fees. Even if there is an interest-free period, it is best to get into the habit of paying on time.

Pay more than the minimum fee. If you can't afford to pay the whole balance, you should pay more than the minimum fee in order to stay out of debt. If you pay only the minimum and the interest increases, you can expect a steady stream of phone calls from credit collectors.

Make sure you understand the payment schedule. Prevent your credit score from falling by paying on time.

Know when you're in over your head. If you can't keep up on your payments, consider credit card consolidation and professional assistance.

An important part of making sure that you're using your credit properly is having a comprehensive plan. When it comes to money, that plan is often referred to as *budgeting*.

You have to look at the amount of money that you take in, decide realistically if you can depend on taking in the same amount of money in the future, and then once you have set aside money for living expenses, establish a plan for saving some of the money and investing the rest.

SAVING VS. INVESTING

The difference between saving and investing depends a lot on the personality and the needs of the individual. If you don't really need the money and you don't foresee any near-term and midterm expenses that are outside of your stable earning capacity, then you might want to invest more since there can be a significant upside to investing.

If you have any uncertainty or level of discomfort about actually needing the money that you have now sometime in the future, because your job is unstable or because your source of income is unreliable, the last thing you want to do is invest. *If you actually need the money for the future, save it—don't invest it.*

One of the worst mistakes that people make is investing in high-risk funds or high-interest investments because they need more money than they are actually taking in. It is just the opposite. If you really need the money, figure out a way to make more money by doing extra work or else tighten your belt and spend less.

Know the Reality of the Risk

Never count on high returns from investments for your lifestyle. Anyone who tells you that high yield doesn't come with high risk is a liar. The entire banking system and the top professionals are not stupid. If there were a way to make substantially above Treasury rates with no risk, everyone would do it.

THE IMPORTANCE OF GOOD RECORD KEEPING

Record keeping, documentation, and the appropriate filings are a necessary part of life both personally and professionally. They are your protection in case something goes wrong, or if you are being held accountable for something that you did. If you don't keep records of what you do, you could be accused of crimes and you have no way of tracking what you actually own.

Record keeping is mandatory in our society. Without record keeping you can't pay your taxes, you can't obtain credit in business situations, and you can't justify to others what you're doing at work. Failure to keep records properly and submit proper filings has brought down many people who simply later forget what they did.

> ## The Consequences of Not Keeping Good Records
>
> *We had a catastrophe in one of our businesses in which a partner of mine kept things in his head instead of keeping proper records. He ended up placing an order that he forgot he had already placed. As a result, the company was faced with too much inventory, which set off a series of problems that destabilized a company that otherwise would have been very healthy.*

You can't rely solely on your memory. First of all, it's not a legal document and can't be used in court. Secondly, there are too many things on your mind for you to remember everything you did. Record keeping, documentation, and filings are a necessary part of life.

SELF-ASSESSMENT QUESTIONS

- What does money mean to you? Do you understand your emotional relationship with money?
- Have you made mistakes managing your money in the past? Can you identify what the mistakes were?
- What is your relationship with time? Do you procrastinate or do you organize your time and use it well?
- Are you single-minded or do you multitask well?
- Do problems scare you? Do you feel competent in addressing the challenges you face?

12

Your
HEALTH,
Improved
Wellness, Balance and Energy

"If I knew I was going to live this long, I'd have taken better care of myself."

—MICKEY MANTLE
Legendary New York Yankee,
Member, National Baseball Hall of Fame

Regardless of what approach you take to health care, caring for your body and mind helps to ensure a long, healthy life, maximum energy, and a positive, attractive outward appearance.

HOLISTIC MEDICINE DEFINED

Holistic medicine is often defined as "relating to or concerned with wholes or with complete systems rather than with the analysis of, treatment of, or dissection into parts."

Essentially, holistic medicine views health as the product of many factors, rather than one problem or symptom.

It is the concept of looking at the whole person and deals not only with the person's wellness, balance and energy, but with all aspects of a person's life. If people are not happy in the workplace or in their personal life, it will have an impact on their health and well-being.

Thus, holistic health encompasses far more than our conventional definition of health: *it takes into account how a person sees him or herself in the world professionally and personally.*

HOLISTIC MEDICINE
VS.
CONVENTIONAL MEDICINE

Today, holistic health care is becoming more widely accepted in the Western medical community and is understood in the broader macro-economic community as being important to society. It is making inroads as both a replacement for and a complement to conventional medicine, and in the broadest sense, as being a benefit to society to ensure good health and a prosperous future for communities.

Examples of the recent acceptance of a holistic approach include awareness of the importance of diet and exercise as a means to prevent obesity and diabetes. Another example is taking more vitamins and supplements and eating well, rather than just taking pharmaceutical drugs. Holistic health care encourages a proactive approach to disease prevention and encourages individuals to play an active role in their health and well-being, rather than relying only on a doctor's care.

Part of the increasing interest in holistic health has to do with the fact that *people are living longer*. With its well-rounded approach, holistic health care is especially beneficial for the treatment of some chronic conditions, many of which afflict people as they age. Western medicine, on the other hand, is often more useful for treating injuries or acute illnesses.

Many health professionals accept that holistic health care is not only beneficial for chronic illness, but also can be used as part of a program of preventative medicine. For many years, some of the finest minds in the medical profession have been advocating the use of preventative medicine instead of waiting to treat diseases after they occur.

TRADITIONAL MEDICINE

When we speak of the impact of holistic health and wellness and its rising popularity, we are speaking mostly of its role in Western culture. In the Far East, many of the techniques of holistic health that are just now becoming popular in the United States have been in use for thousands of years. In fact, what we call "holistic" medicine here is in fact considered as traditional, widely practiced medicine by the majority of people in the world.

A Cynic's Viewpoint?

Cynics have argued that the reason the medical community has not embraced preventative medicine is because there is no way to charge for it on the same basis as Western medicine. As the health care system in the United States becomes an overwhelming, costly burden on our society's ability to be able to compete in global markets, holistic health care has gained popularity not only among the population and the medical community but in the political establishment as well. It is a proactive approach to health that will save money and time.

BE GRATEFUL FOR YOUR BODY

There is an ancient proverb, "I cried because I had no shoes, until I met a man who had no feet." Part of being well in mind and body includes being grateful for your ability to function on a healthy level. If more people understood this concept they would be a lot happier. In a way, happiness is not having the things that you like, but *liking and appreciating the things that you have.*

A Valuable Lesson

At an early age I was in an accident that prevented me from walking. Before I entered kindergarten I had physical therapy, but walking was still a struggle. In a sense, I regard that as one of the most fortunate events in my life. It gave me the discipline to focus and appreciate how good it feels to be healthy. Most people don't get the opportunity to understand how valuable it is to be able to walk and live as a healthy person. They sometimes find out later in life when they are injured or have a disease, and often it is too late for them to appreciate the gift of good health. Never take anything for granted.

"HOW-TO" GUIDE TO WELLNESS

The goal of this chapter is to explore approaches and strategies to achieving wellness. With total wellness, you will become more energized in the workplace and increase your productivity. Such a transformation will positively impact the way others perceive you and, in turn, can translate into achieving greater success in all aspects of your life.

To provide you with an overview of holistic health, I divide it into three categories: *knowledge, attitude* and *practice.* You should follow up on your own through books and the Internet to learn how to achieve holistic wellness in your life.

> *Knowledge* is required so that you can have facts on which to base your plan. Of course, this book cannot possibly give you all the specifics you need on how to achieve the full spectrum of holistic wellness; that would take volumes. Instead, *The SELF, Improved* will provide you with general guidelines. From here on, you can read articles and look into other sources to increase your knowledge in the areas that specifically interest you.

> A right *attitude* is also key. There are plenty of books on nutrition, exercise and health-related practices that you can read, but the most important thing is to have a positive attitude based on what you can accomplish and *give yourself enough time in order to travel the path to wellness.*

> Finally, and perhaps most important, you must put your new plan for health into *practice.* This chapter will provide you with tips on the best ways to get started— and how to continue for a lifetime.

NUTRITION AND ENVIRONMENT

The most important aspect of holistic health care is an understanding of how nutrition affects wellness.

The saying, "You are what you eat," is in fact quite accurate. Science has proven that the way our bodies, and in turn, our minds, function, is largely influenced by what we eat and drink. Proper nutrition is one of the key factors that link health, fitness and overall well-being. The body is a very complex machine and physiological system that will not function properly without the proper fuel. Food is broken down in the body to provide energy and the life-sustaining elements your body needs.

Perhaps one of the most revealing examples of the saying, "You are what you eat," can be found in the latest studies on diet and children.

THE EVIDENCE:
A RISE IN DIABETES AND OBESITY

Studies have shown that students in grade school who don't get proper nutrition during the day cannot learn as well as students who receive a well-balanced, nutritious diet.

Outside of school, people with low incomes often choose foods high in carbohydrates because they are the least expensive, but are still filling.

In the United States, the number of overweight children ages 6 to 11 has increased over 200 percent from 1980 to 2006. From ages 12 to 19, the number of overweight children has increased over 300 percent.

Improper nutrition and obesity not only affects the body's well-being in a physical sense, but also has psychological effects, which can stay with children into their teen years and adulthood. It has been shown that children raised with poor dietary habits develop fat cells that can stay in their system for the rest of their lives. *This will place them in an endless battle for weight control.*

These examples serve to remind us that nutrition plays a key role for all of us from a very early age.

Young Minds

For many years people thought that those from poorer minority groups were not capable of learning. Of course, this was a generalization that was used to perpetuate a stereotype. Now we know that in those cases where children from poorer backgrounds exhibited less aptitude, it was due in large part to an improper diet.

Without the right nutrition, children can and will have difficulty learning. This is why school lunch programs were originally set up: so that students who didn't have proper nutrition at home could at least be reached by some governmental organization. Unfortunately, as economics began to dominate the workplace, schools and governmental agencies, less expensive foods that are high in carbohydrates and low in protein became staples. Soft drinks were being served in schools.

It is only with the recent awareness of the need for proper nutrition as part of a holistic wellness program that changes have been ordered to reduce the amount of sugar that is given to children. Part of this change is the result of the enormous increase in teenage diabetes.

EATING WELL AT WORK

By the time most of us are adults, we have a basic knowledge of what we should and shouldn't eat. However, we still tend to break the rules. Nowhere is this truer than in the workplace.

Like schools, many workplace cafeterias serve cheaper, unhealthy foods to keep meals affordable. Processed foods and carbohydrates in institutional food may save money, but they have little nutritional benefit.

Look carefully at what your workplace cafeteria has to offer and make a decision as to whether or not the food provided can fit into your diet plan. If not, you could speak to the institution's management and see if they have any flexibility. If they cannot work with you, you can always bring food from home or order it from outside establishments where better menu choices are available.

Your nutrition and the nutrition of those around you is important from a very early age. Many of us actually know what is good for us and yet, for added convenience, we eat fast foods, snack foods, sugar and soft drinks, candy and other things that we know are not good for us. Making healthy choices as soon as possible is important. Once you give up these types of foods you actually will lose your taste for them.

WORKING LUNCHES AND DINNER MEETINGS

Going out to lunch or dinner for business is always difficult to fit in with a diet plan. For one thing, these meals very often take more time than is actually required for you to eat what your body needs. When food is in front of you for longer amounts of time, you end up eating it just because it's there.

Breaking Bread

Another challenging part about meetings that take place during meals is that, to a certain extent, breaking bread is part of the socialization process that goes back to ancient times. In other words, we are quite comfortable eating and talking. I used to go out to business dinners and eat a tremendous amount of bread and butter before, during, and after the meal. It just felt natural to eat and talk.

But, of course, you really don't have to eat to participate in a conversation! Make it a rule to always look at what you're eating and try, in your own mind, to count the calories or carbs. When you do this, it will help you make sure to stop eating so many rolls and butter.

GETTING STARTED WITH GOOD NUTRITION

Things are gradually starting to change. Now that our society is more aware of how vital proper nutrition is, changes are taking place to reduce the amount of sugar that is in everyone's diet.

Plan for Wellness

If we carefully plan our eating program, we can eat healthy no matter what our budget is. Oftentimes the proof of this is clear when we look at how other cultures eat.

Many cultures adopted diets with less meat simply because meat was not widely available. This is one of the reasons why Chinese cuisine, for example, features much less meat than an American diet does. In the United States, a 16-ounce steak is considered a reasonable portion for one person to consume. But a Chinese individual not accustomed to eating large amounts of meat could use that 16-ounce steak to feed a table of 20 people!

We can change our eating habits, too.

One of the first things that you have to do when learning to eat well is inform yourself about nutrition. Then, you need to identify an eating program that suits your needs.

When setting up your own personal discipline for practicing wellness, allow room for flexibility within your plan but *create objectives you know you can achieve.*

THE IMPORTANCE OF NUTRITIONAL LABELS

Without knowledge of what you're eating and the amount of fat, carbohydrates and calories involved, eating is almost like gambling.

A Wake-Up Call

Nutritional labeling had a profound effect on me when it first began to appear in restaurants.

Before the caloric content of food was listed, I used to go into Kentucky Fried Chicken® and order a bucket for myself. Then, when they actually listed the amount of calories, I was so horrified by what I had been consuming that I never went back to a Kentucky Fried Chicken. Kentucky Fried Chicken is a great brand and there is nothing wrong with their product, but there was definitely something wrong with the way I was consuming their product. So, for me, I decided to stay away. Nutritional labeling reminds me of exactly what I'm about to consume, and it helps me take actions that are best for myself.

Casinos take the extra step of making you take your money and turn it into chips. As long as you're playing with chips, it doesn't feel like real money.

It's like that with potato chips. Remember the Lays® Potato Chip line: "Betcha can't eat just one!" They were right, you can keep eating them and eating them, and all of a sudden you look at the bag and see that not only was that a lot of calories, but that bag of potato chips might have contained 16 servings, and you just ate the whole thing. If you don't do anything to burn those calories, they will "convert" to excess fat in your body and you will gain weight.

Really look at the labeling and make a point of being aware of what it says. Do the division and figure out how much of your daily caloric allotment you're really going to eat if you consume that meal. Then, make a decision about whether or not you really want to consume it.

Focus on Calorie Content

Sometimes when I go to a Starbucks® and order a cup of coffee, I think maybe I'll have a muffin or a piece of pound cake. But when I look at the calorie content and see that the muffin is 400 or 500 calories, I often then decide that I'll just have a cup of coffee. Looking at the calorie count is a "shock to the system" and a wake-up call that can encourage you to make good decisions. It's extremely important.

Becoming knowledgeable about nutritional labeling is really about empowering you to make good decisions. The purpose of this book is not to be judgmental. If somebody consciously decides that they want to eat an entire bag of potato chips or a quart of ice cream and they know what the consequences will be, then there's no problem.

But that's not what usually happens.

What usually happens for most of us is that we consume food without knowing or thinking about what we're doing. Then, we pay the price. *And that price can be very high.*

A bad diet doesn't just lead to obesity but, over time, it can lead to disease. For example, gaining weight is not just unattractive; it can lead to serious chronic disease such as:

- Coronary heart disease
- Type 2 diabetes
- Cancers (endometrial, breast and colon)
- Hypertension (high blood pressure)
- Dyslipidemia (for example, high total cholesterol or high levels of triglycerides)
- Stroke
- Liver and gallbladder disease
- Sleep apnea and respiratory problems
- Osteoarthritis (a degeneration of cartilage and its underlying bone within a joint)
- Gynecological problems (abnormal menses, infertility)

BEWARE OF SUGAR

Many of us have developed a taste for sugar. Although, for the most part, we know what is good for us, we continue to eat foods that are convenient, including fast foods, snack foods, soft drinks, candy, and others. Unfortunately, some industries have set up research centers, like the Sugar Association, that tell us sugar is great. *This we know is not true.*

The good news about sugar is that if you stay away from it long enough you will most likely lose your taste for it so that when you finally do eat something with sugar, it will taste too sweet, you won't like it, and you will cease to crave it. This is all the more reason why making adjustments to diet as soon as possible is important. Then, if we keep at it and maintain self-control for a given period of time, our bodies will become accustomed to healthy food and, in this way, our cravings will adapt to our healthier diet.

Getting Rid of Sugar

Taking sugar completely out of your diet, in my opinion, would be a good move. On this point, I can't say I practice what I preach, but I know myself and I know that saying, "I'll never have sugar again," is an unrealistic objective for me. I don't want to be fanatical about anything. So, I haven't given up desserts because I believe that it would not be a long-term diet that I would want to live with. Similarly, I haven't given up drinks; alcohol has an extremely high caloric content (drinking beer or other liquors has to go into your equation, since alcohol has a lot of calories). Although I haven't eliminated my sugar consumption entirely, I've reduced my levels of sugar. I also use artificial sweeteners in coffee and other beverages or meals where real sugar is not a necessity for me. In this way I do practice what I preach: I'm realistic about what I can and can't go without, and I set my objectives so they are realistic for me.

CASE STUDY: THE ATKINS DIET

Dr. Atkins taught us that a lot of what we learned about weight from our parents was untrue. He told us we could eat all the fat we wanted and not gain weight as long as we stayed away from complex carbohydrates and sugar. Everything about the Atkins diet was counterintuitive.

The Diet That's Not for Everyone

I knew Dr. Atkins and tried the Atkins diet. For a period of time it was very successful but ultimately I learned that it was not going be a helpful long-term diet for me. It required a tremendous amount of self-discipline. When I first tried the diet, I was amazed that it worked. But I was even more amazed when I went to dinner with Dr. Atkins and discovered that not only was he overweight, but that even he had problems following his own routine!

People who followed the Atkins diet were stunned to find out that they could eat an enormous amount of fat and not gain weight. This works because, with the Atkins diet, you have to be fanatical about avoiding carbohydrates.

However, when people cheated on Atkins and had a doughnut or a piece of cake, all that fat and the sudden reintroduction of carbohydrates into their system made them gain more weight than they would have if they had maintained a healthy balance of carbohydrates and fats.

So what was wrong with the diet? One of the proven health issues was that a high protein, no carbohydrate diet created kidney problems for many people. Beyond that, the most difficult issue to address was that it required behavior that was unrealistic for most people. As long as you were on it and didn't cheat it would work; but if you cheated, you would gain back the weight.

Bottom line: don't choose an eating program that has unrealistic objectives.

THE GOAL OF EATING WELL:
TOTAL HEALTH

There is something else that we all have to understand when we choose a diet. *It's not all about weight.*

Eating well is also about energy and proper health. People who are anorexic may not have a weight problem, but they sure have a health problem. *Anorexics are not healthy.* Being stick thin is not a good goal. You need balance and to take a sense of pleasure from your life, how you eat, and how you exercise.

Beware of Sports Drinks

One of the problems with the sports drinks advertised on television is that when people watch the ad from their couch, they don't realize that their bodies and the body of the athlete on TV are functioning under a totally different set of circumstances. Obviously, watching TV is nothing like playing the sport! Therefore, if you drink sports drinks without working out, you will quickly discover that instead of their giving you the extra electrolytes and carbohydrates that you need for intense play, you end up gaining a lot of weight.

When you choose an eating plan you may want to work with your doctor and make a list of what your realistic level of activity is going to be to go along with that diet. If you're really serious about it, you may want to have blood tests and make sure you're healthy before you go on a diet that may affect your electrolyte balance, blood pressure or other physiological functions. If you are in good health and you know the amount of exercise that you can do, then pick a diet that will be sustainable and keep you in shape.

CHOOSING AN EATING PLAN

There are thousands of eating plans that you are barraged with every day through TV, advertising, and magazines. How do you determine which one is right for you? Just like Alice in Wonderland, who needed to decide which path to take, where you want to go *depends upon your individual objectives.*

Activity Determines Caloric Intake

During the 2008 Olympics, everyone was talking about how much Michael Phelps, the great swimmer, consumed. The number of calories was off the charts! However, the average person did not understand that these calories were required for him to perform physically, and that, without his strenuous training program to burn those calories, he would have gained a tremendous amount of weight. But because he balanced his caloric needs with his exercise requirements, he was in top physical condition. Athletes often gain a lot of weight when they stop exercising rigorously because they don't realize that they have to immediately lower their calorie input to accommodate their new, slower metabolism.

Advice from Experts

GUIDELINES FOR
GOOD HEALTH AND NUTRITION

Aim for a healthy weight that is realistic for you.

Be physically active each day.

Choose a variety of grains, in particular whole grains.

Choose a variety of fruits and vegetables.

Choose a diet low in saturated fat and cholesterol and moderate in total fat.

Choose beverages and foods that are not high in sugar.

Choose and prepare foods with less salt.

Drink alcoholic beverages only in moderation.

In addition to healthy nutrition, you might want to look at nutraceuticals and herbal supplements. Nutraceuticals are food products that, when used regularly and in a preventative manner, may have the beneficial effects of pharmaceuticals. The FDA has decided not to regulate nutraceuticals or herbal supplements despite the fact that the general population is now taking these products in greater amounts than pharmaceuticals, and some of these products have contraindications with Western medicine.

Neutral on Nutraceuticals

I do not take a position with respect to nutraceuticals or herbal supplements. Some people have found that these products have enormous benefits. Some doctors believe that they have no benefits. There is no doubt that certain herbal remedies that have been developed over the course of thousands of years, and used as part of traditional Chinese medicine and in other cultures, have value. But the ongoing disputes as to where these products come from and the lack of controls placed on them by a health agency mean that you have to buy these products from people who you know are very knowledgeable and reputable.

HEALTH AT HOME

Health at home is first controlled by what you bring into your house. Don't keep things in your house that are not on your diet, unless you're entertaining for others. There is no point in tempting yourself; if it's not in your house you're less likely to eat it.

Make a point of shopping healthy—that's half the trick of eating healthy. Get into a routine of buying healthy foods that fit the diet that you picked out. Keep a list of healthy recipes on hand for things you like and develop a regimen that works for your available free time. Home is an easy place to control your eating.

The most important thing to remember is to always be conscious of what you're doing. Very often somebody can be on a diet and watch all their calories and then they get on the telephone in the evening, have an upsetting conversation, and eat an entire quart of ice cream. This is the type of unconscious behavior that will throw off your diet and your wellness. The key to success is to always be conscious of what you put in your mouth. Use willpower in combination with healthy action.

PHYSICAL FITNESS

When you put a plan for health into practice, that plan must involve exercise. Without exercise, proper diet is not going to create a healthy body. Exercise of any kind will improve your overall energy level. Used in conjunction with a healthy diet and a balanced program, you will feel more energized.

Exercise stimulates the mind and body. All types of exercise require some degree of concentration on things other than your daily routine. This provides a break from the mundane things in your life. Exercise is a timeout where you can choose the type of activity you want to do and strengthen your body in the image that you want to share with others, and one that will make you feel good.

As noted in the book *Combat Fat! The Complete Plan for Permanent Weight Loss* by Andrew Flach, RoseMarie Alfieri, M. Laurel Cutlip, RD, LN, Stew Smith, and James Villepigue, incorporating an exercise routine into your life and building a healthier body means that you will also burn calories when you are at rest. The book states, "The leaner you are, the more fat you will be burning each and every day, even when you are not exercising."

Exercise is the key to ensuring that your body performs at optimum level.

THERE IS NO SHORTCUT

There are a lot of ads on TV and in print that sell "magic exercisers" that promise to do the work for you. Most of these claims are not true. The adage, "no pain, no gain" is true to a certain extent. For some of us, exercising may not seem pleasurable, but it is something that we have to do to achieve wellness.

To maintain that higher energy level, determine the best means of exercise for you. It doesn't matter if you exercise alone, with a friend, or at a gym—what matters is that you exercise.

AN ALTERNATIVE APPROACH TO PHYSICAL FITNESS

Depending on what your goals are in terms of your physique, you may want to consider a more unconventional approach to physical fitness. What do I mean by this? Eastern arts and meditation, yoga, tai chi and martial arts all require concentration as well as physical discipline and strength. In yoga, for example, you can train your mind and your body at the same time: by using positions to help you be aware of using your muscles, you can build strength and relax your mind.

Unlike Western training, yoga and other forms of Eastern meditation don't build bulky muscles. Instead, they create lean muscle and build flexibility. Muscle bulk and muscle building come with progressive weight resistance. You need your muscles to work against weight on a progressive basis in order to build bulk and muscle mass.

Again, muscles are an indicator of fitness, but building muscle just for the sake of it can be a dangerous goal. The desire to develop muscles has led many to steroid use. This is a really bad idea—not only are these drugs illegal, but they will make you less healthy later in life. Be sure that you exercise in a way that is right for your body and choose a means of working out that will guard your health for the future.

The Importance of Good Form

Unfortunately, many runners who thought that they were exercising in order to stay healthy over the long term and keep themselves in shape, found out that they were using the wrong sneakers or poor form and, because of this, developed problems (arthritis, back pain, knee problems and chronic joint pain).

CHOOSING AN EXERCISE PROGRAM

Some people exercise because they want to relax or "turn off" their thoughts, in which case Eastern physical arts will probably be their preference. Still others want to look athletic and strong. As we said in earlier chapters, what program you choose depends upon what you want for yourself. If you want to project an image of being muscular, Western physical arts will give you the bulk. No matter what you choose, act responsibly. You do this by setting realistic goals for yourself.

With regular practice you will be able to develop your own personal program of physical arts that is related specifically to your own needs.

MOTIVATION

An exercise routine is one of the hardest things to maintain. Depending on where you live it may be much harder than any other program. If you live in an urban area and you have to go to a gym, you have to *make* the time to go. This can be very difficult. That's why some people use personal trainers. Personal trainers are people who force you to ignore your distractions, to take the time to keep the appointment, and stick with your schedule.

You can always create a reason not to exercise, the same way you created reasons not to do homework when you were a kid. There's always a reason to put something off. That is why we have to manage our time. And in the management of time we have to create time each day for exercise. If you need to, use charts and schedules, personal trainers, classes—anything that helps structure your time—so that you can develop a routine that helps you meet your objective.

Selling Motivation

In the mid-'70s I developed the Muscle Worker®, which was the first hydraulic exerciser, later referred to as the Bruce Jenner Exerciser. It became one of the biggest products in the exercise business at that time. But even then I understood that the purpose of any exercise equipment is really more motivational than necessity. Anyone can do push-ups, sit-ups or go running on their own. It doesn't take an exerciser to keep you in shape; it takes discipline and the allocation of time.

COMMITTING TO AN EXERCISE PLAN

The most important thing in planning a training program, whether it's in Eastern or Western arts, is to stick to the schedule that you make. If you decide that you're going to do yoga, tai chi, repetitions, or running, the most important thing is to make sure that you make up a schedule that you can keep. You can join a gym with fancy equipment, but it won't do you any good if you only go every day the first week and then find yourself skipping one day, then two, then three.

It's better to exercise for 10 or 15 minutes a few days a week, and build on that gradually over time, than it is to schedule an hour a day and quit after the first week.

You need to set up a schedule that's realistic and that you can commit to. Those who have full-time jobs, family obligations, school schedules, or other time constraints will have to create a realistic schedule they can stick to.

Only you know how important wellness and holistic health are to you, and only you can then decide how much time you want to allocate to them. Everyone has their own set of criteria and trying to force other people's criteria on ourselves doesn't work. *That is the basis of this book: to choose what works for you personally.*

Most people have difficulty sustaining an organized program or routine over time. This is human nature and it is the enemy.

Health Clubs

One of the ways that health clubs make a lot of money is to sell annual memberships. They do this knowing that most people will drop out early. They are able to give tremendous discounts because they bank on the fact that you will not be able to pace yourself and that you are going to drop out of the program.

This is an example of how human nature can work against our best intentions. But you can reverse the statistics and commit to health no matter what.

THE RIGHT ATTITUDE: BODY AND MIND

Holistic health, wellness and balance are as much psychological as physiological.

Although martial artists are portrayed in film as being violent, the physical accomplishments that come with the practice are largely based upon the discipline of the mind. While proper conditioning and proper health care, and good diet and exercise are important to holistic health, probably the most important factor in health is your mindset and the determination to be healthy.

A FITTER MIND:
STRESS REDUCTION

In addition to practicing proper nutrition and exercise, many of us need to utilize techniques for stress reduction and relaxation. Our way of life has become very complex, and with that complexity comes an unbelievable amount of stress. Controlling that stress is important to maintaining your balance in the world.

IDENTIFYING THE SOURCE OF STRESS

The first step to controlling stress is to identify its source. The purpose of stress reduction and relaxation techniques is to understand what causes you pressure and to then control it.

Thoughts that create stress can either come from a real or a perceived dilemma or situation. Regardless of the source, we can always lower our level of stress to some degree. Obviously soldiers in the battlefield and other people in demanding situations cannot avoid all stress, no matter what technique they use. But, for most of us, we can limit things that cause us to feel anxious or tense.

The Danger of Too Much Stress

Stress left unattended can actually cause many physiological dysfunctions. Years ago people used to refer to these as psychosomatic diseases. The term "psychosomatic" became synonymous in some people's minds with "imaginary." This was a mistake. Psychosomatic diseases are as real as any other disease, and they often cause measurable physiological dysfunctions that are as detrimental as any illness.

Very often, we cannot eliminate the source of stress. In these cases, our job then becomes to control our reaction to the stress. Biofeedback, meditation, breathing exercises, choosing healthy thoughts and attitudes and other methods are useful. All these approaches have one thing in common. *They teach us to pay attention to our stress and control our bodies so we can put ourselves in a more relaxed state.*

BIOFEEDBACK AND SELF-AWARENESS

Biofeedback uses an assortment of instruments to monitor bodily functions and relay them to the participant in real time so that he or she can understand the subliminal workings of his or her own body. The theory is that understanding how your body works when you are not controlling it will allow you to remain relaxed, no matter what your situation may be.

Biofeedback equipment allows us to measure different functions, such as heart rate or peripheral body temperature. In this way, biofeedback allows people to actually *see* how they are reducing stress. This is useful because it is believed that seeing your heart rate increase or decrease actually enables the mind to reduce stress. Essentially, the mind can control the body.

The Complexity of the Human Mind

The mind is wonderfully complex. For example, if the brain didn't coordinate with our optical system in the way it does, our eyes would actually show us the world upside down. In order for us to see properly, the optical system needs to be interpreted by the brain, which inverts everything right side up so that we can function.

For those of you who have never tried biofeedback, it can be a fascinating and useful tool and one that will serve you well on your path to health. Although it may seem too good to be true, it works. Sigmund Freud, one of the pioneers in the field of psychoanalysis, realized that having people understand what was at the root of their problem usually helped them solve that problem.

Biofeedback is one way that you can come to understand the root cause of your stress. Then you can take steps to stop it.

COMPONENTS OF RELAXATION

In *The Relaxation Response*, authors Herbert Benson and Miriam Z. Klipper describe their discovery that, much in the same way that our bodies respond to stress in a physical way, by releasing adrenaline or inducing a "fight or flight" response, our bodies can also respond to relaxation in a physical way. To obtain this state, the authors recommend following the steps listed below:

1. Find a quiet environment.
2. Use a mental device—a sound, word, phrase, or prayer repeated silently or aloud, or a fixed gaze at an object.

3. Have a passive attitude—not worrying about how well you are performing the technique and simply putting aside distracting thoughts to return to your focus.
4. Sit in a comfortable position.

IDENTIFYING WELLNESS GOALS

So, out of the vast universe of holistic programs and techniques, how do you decide which one is right for you? You start at the beginning, you look at as many as possible, and you set priorities and determine what is most important to you. Ask the question: *What are my particular needs for wellness, balance and energy?*

Remember to prioritize your efforts based on your individual lifestyle. Some people are lucky and don't have a weight problem. Although these individuals should still eat healthfully, they do not have to diet. Other people have to find a diet that they can live with, and follow it, in order to maintain a healthy weight. People who are athletes are going to spend more time on exercise because they are motivated to excel at a given sport. Others don't care about sports or athletics and need to find motivation in another way.

This is where balance comes in. No matter what your body type is, you still need to make wise food choices. And, even if you don't care about sports or athletics, you still need to exercise at a minimal level in order to keep your body healthy. No one can do everything, so set your priorities carefully.

SET REALISTIC GOALS

Trying to do everything plus maintain a job and a personal life is not going to increase your efficiency—it's going to get you frustrated and you'll end up doing none of it. Therefore, once you've set up your priorities, make sure that they're practical. Self-discipline in wellness is going to be very much related to your priorities and your realistic objectives. Without realistic objectives you will not succeed in self-discipline.

If you aim to lose 20 pounds in seven days, you're not going to accomplish anything. If you want to exercise 2 hours every day you probably won't do it. On your personal path to wellness balance and energy, the word "balance" becomes very important. Determine how important the various factors we've discussed in *The SELF, Improved* are to you and then make sure you do at least the minimal amount required in each area.

In any program, whether it is weight loss, exercise, stress reduction or any form of self-improvement, developing realistic goals that are consistent with your objectives is the most important place to start. If you set your expectations too high, you're not going to be able to keep up with the pace and you're going to drop out of the program.

For most of us, self-discipline can be a challenging undertaking. That's why a lot of people find it very difficult to work at home. Today with computers, telephones and videoconferencing, a lot of people could operate out of their homes, but the self-discipline that it takes is very difficult. Therefore we create work environments that insulate people from the day-to-day activities, not because it helps them function, but that it keeps them away from daily distractions.

YOUR PLAN

Now that you know where you want to go, you need to make sure you can get there. You do so by making a plan. To begin, spend some time researching titles at a bookstore or your library that address your specific goals as regards diet, wellness and exercise. You can also research on the Internet, speak to your doctor, or consult family and friends for direction. Craft a routine that will allow you to eat well, to exercise more, to reduce stress and generally become healthier. All of this can make you feel better about yourself and allow you to control your own body.

SELF-ASSESSMENT QUESTIONS

- Do you incorporate any holistic health care in your life?
- Do you pay attention to what you eat or do you grab food on the run without thinking?
- Do you exercise?
- How do you manage stress? Do you have a strategy for stress management?

FINAL
SELF-ASSESSMENTS

Now that you've come to the book's conclusion you have better insight into your own strengths and weaknesses. So it is a good time to re-assess!

You may discover that you are better in some areas than you originally indicated in Chart I. Or you may realize where you should concentrate your efforts so that you become more effective in your career or personal life. Once again, fill out the following charts as objectively as possible. Do certain Attributes hold the same importance to you as you previously indicated? Are your priorities and goals the same as before?

Take the time to go back over the first three charts that you completed before you read the book and compare responses. You may be surprised.

CHART VI:
PERSONAL REASSESSMENT

On a scale of 1 to 10, in your opinion only, how do you rate yourself on these traits now?

Go down the entire list and put a number after each attribute. (1 = not good at all and 10 = the very best.)

You can give the same rating to more than one trait.

Your honest opinion of yourself	
ATTRIBUTES/TRAITS	Rate each item on a scale of 1-10
Overall Appearance	
Dress Well/Nice Clothing	
Healthy Weight	
Hair	
Grooming	
Facial Appearance—Skin/Makeup	
Overall Physical Carriage	
Posture	
Body Language	
Open/Confident/Poised	
Strong/Vibrant/Energetic	
Overall Communication Skills	
Speech	
Writing	
Good Listener	
Clarity	
Speaking in Public	
Overall Intelligence and Aptitude	
Educated	
Experienced	
Street Smart	
Talented	
Well-Versed in Current Affairs	
Good with Numbers and Math	
Read and Write Well	
Overall Personality	
Confident	
Ambitious/Motivated	
Serious/Reliable	
Friendly/Happy	
Caring/Considerate/Tolerant	
Patient	
Relate Well to Others	
Cool Under Pressure or Stress	
Overall Professional Skills	
Leadership	
Organized	
Multi-Tasker/Time Management	
Preparedness	
Motivator	
Computer Ability	
Clear Thinker	
Overall Etiquette	
Personal Manners	
Business Manners	
Overall Health	
Physically Fit	
Eat Well	
Sleep Well	
Strong/Vibrant/Energetic	

CHART VII:
IMPORTANCE RATINGS

On a scale of 1 to 10, in your opinion only, now that you have completed the book, how important are these traits to you?

Don't consider other people's values— only your own. What attributes do you admire most and wish for in your own life?

(1 = not at all important and 10 = the most important.)

Rate them all. You can give the same rating to more than one trait.

How important are these traits to you?

ATTRIBUTES/TRAITS	Rate each item on a scale of 1-10
Overall Appearance	
Dress Well/Nice Clothing	
Healthy Weight	
Hair	
Grooming	
Facial Appearance—Skin/Makeup	
Overall Physical Carriage	
Posture	
Body Language	
Open/Confident/Poised	
Strong/Vibrant/Energetic	
Overall Communication Skills	
Speech	
Writing	
Good Listener	
Clarity	
Speaking in Public	
Overall Intelligence and Aptitude	
Educated	
Experienced	
Street Smart	
Talented	
Well-Versed in Current Affairs	
Good with Numbers and Math	
Read and Write Well	
Overall Personality	
Confident	
Ambitious/Motivated	
Serious/Reliable	
Friendly/Happy	
Caring/Considerate/Tolerant	
Patient	
Relate Well to Others	
Cool Under Pressure or Stress	
Overall Professional Skills	
Leadership	
Organized	
Multi-Tasker/Time Management	
Preparedness	
Motivator	
Computer Ability	
Clear Thinker	
Overall Etiquette	
Personal Manners	
Business Manners	
Overall Health	
Physically Fit	
Eat Well	
Sleep Well	
Strong/Vibrant/Energetic	

CHART VIII:
PERSONAL ATTRIBUTE PRIORITIES

Do you currently possess the attributes you admire and think are important? Do you have them at the level you believe you should? Remember, you can always improve!

To identify your goals and priorities, subtract your Importance Rating (Column B) from your Personal Rating (Column A).

Any Negative (-) number indicates the need for some work on your part. The lower the number, the more you need to focus on improving this attribute.

Copy your answers from the re-assessments in Charts VI and VII on the previous pages to calculate your priorities.

ATTRIBUTES/TRAITS	A. YOUR HONEST OPINION OF YOURSELF (copy from previous chart VI)	B. HOW IMPORTANT ARE THESE TRAITS TO YOU? (copy from previous chart VII)	A – B = C (+ or -) Negative #'s are your Priorities
Overall Appearance			
Dress Well/Nice Clothing			
Healthy Weight			
Hair			
Grooming			
Facial Appearance—Skin/Makeup			
Overall Physical Carriage			
Posture			
Body Language			
Open/Confident/Poised			
Strong/Vibrant/Energetic			
Overall Communication Skills			
Speech			
Writing			
Good Listener			
Clarity			
Speaking in Public			
Overall Intelligence and Aptitude			
Educated			
Experienced			
Street Smart			
Talented			
Well-Versed in Current Affairs			
Good with Numbers and Math			
Read and Write Well			
Overall Personality			
Confident			
Ambitious/Motivated			
Serious/Reliable			
Friendly/Happy			
Caring/Considerate/Tolerant			
Patient			
Relate Well to Others			
Cool Under Pressure or Stress			
Overall Professional Skills			
Leadership			
Organized			
Multi-Tasker/Time Management			
Preparedness			
Motivator			
Computer Ability			
Clear Thinker			
Overall Etiquette			
Personal Manners			
Business Manners			
Overall Health			
Physically Fit			
Eat Well			
Sleep Well			
Strong/Vibrant/Energetic			

THE FINAL WORD

Understanding your strengths and weaknesses and developing the best balance for your life is what this book is about. It's not about someone else's life; it's about your own life. The Science of Self-Improvement and the assessments act as a sophisticated mirror to let you look at yourself from many different angles and determine how you want to present yourself to others.

The SELF, Improved will teach you about managing behavioral objectives and getting what you want out of meetings, relationships and all human interactions. From those who are just learning how to portray themselves, to the highest level leaders of industry, the tools discussed in this book can help you see yourself as you are perceived by others. It is a more powerful mirror that reflects back to you your total self. Then you can choose the person you want to be.

"The best revenge is massive success."
—FRANK SINATRA
International Music and Acting Legend

Epilogue

by Debbie Joffe Ellis
Licensed Mental Health Counselor
Widow and Collaborator of World Famous
20th Century Psychologist, Dr. Albert Ellis

Life is great.

Despite its challenges, and the necessity to endure loss, disappointment, and grief at times, we can also experience much joy. And whether our circumstances are good and harmonious or not, the potential for even greater fulfillment abounds... if we are willing to do what it takes to create it. Let's choose to do so!

How can we do this?

Awareness is the key, and the vital first step on the journey toward fulfillment, empowerment and choice. By taking a good hard look at ourselves and what we do, we can recognize that which is life-enhancing, and that which is self-defeating and against our self-interest.

The SELF, Improved helps us do just that.

It is important to be conscious of our goals and to create those which are realistic and do-able. This book encourages us to

237

clarify our goals—or to create new ones. With awareness of actions that will maximize the attainment of these goals, we can then explore the best choices and the "how-to's" of carrying them out. Again, this book helps us define our direction on this path.

Albert Ellis, the great pioneering psychologist who was the creator of Rational Emotive Behavior Therapy and the father of cognitive psychology, pointed out that we humans are constructivists: in large part, we create our lives, behaviors and emotions. If we recognize the flaws and faults of our own doing, we can then "deconstruct" what we have done—and construct anew!

Remembering this can give us hope when we feel stuck or unfulfilled.

Be aware, be clear about your goals, and take the necessary steps and actions to manifest them.

The self-assessment charts and self-assessment questions throughout this book are helpful tools which can greatly assist us in recognizing the status quo of our lives, in order that we might, when necessary, make fresh decisions about changes, so that we can determine whether we are doing as much as we can to maximize satisfaction and success in our lives. Different areas for self-discovery and assessment are presented in *The SELF, Improved.*

We are not our image. Our image is not our soul, spirit or essence. But it is an external presentation that—when well thought-out, appropriate and carried out beautifully—can often be of significant help in attaining certain goals. This book offers information about image that is worth contemplating and acting upon.

We humans are largely social animals, so it is most helpful to learn to maximize communication skills in all areas, including presentation, writing and social interactions.

This book provides tools to help us do this.

For comfort, energy, vitality and well-being in life, good health is necessary. Understanding the mind-body connection and the influences of good (and deficient) nutrition is most important. Even if we have a pre-existing condition or an inherited predisposition for developing certain ailments, the greater our knowledge and related actions, the greater the possibility for prevention, reduced symptoms or cure. This book encourages us to seek appropriate and sound knowledge, and explores some strategies for wellness.

It is important in life to keep things in perspective, to think in ways that create healthy emotions, and to maintain realistic optimism and hope. Making mistakes, failing to achieve some goals and experiencing disappointment are natural aspects of the process of living.

If we refuse to depress ourselves when things don't go as we wish—and instead learn from these experiences in order to keep going and try new approaches—then we are empowered and victorious humans. Success does not only come from attaining our goals—it also comes from not allowing ourselves to feel defeated when we do not attain them. Remember, as Albert Ellis taught, to always unconditionally accept yourself—even if some of your ventures fail. If you fail or make mistakes, *you* are not a failure or mistake. You just failed at something you did. No tragedy. Cultivate a loving relationship with yourself.

Use the material in this book to help you as much as possible. Let *The SELF, Improved* encourage ongoing self-awareness and good actions for change when change is called for.

Accept that life is not always fair and we don't always get what we want—and keep going and experimenting anyway! In so doing, you can play the game of life, creating and recreating your life with relish.

Enjoy yourself and, as Albert Ellis would say, "Have a ball!"

Bibliography

Alred, Gerald J., Charles T. Brusaw and Walter E. Oliu, *The Business Writer's Handbook*, 8th ed., New York: St. Martin's Press, Inc., 2006.

Benson, Herbert and Miriam Z. Klipper, *The Relaxation Response*, New York: HarperCollins, 2000.

Bixler, Susan and Lisa Scherrer Dugan, *5 Steps to Professional Presence, How to Project Confidence, Competence, and Credibility at Work*, Avon, MA: Adams Media, 2001.

Bolles, Richard Nelson, *What Color is Your Parachute? 2005: A Practical Manual for Job-Hunters and Career-Changers*, Berkeley, CA: Ten Speed Press, 2005.

Carroll, Lewis, *Alice's Adventures in Wonderland*, New York: Harper Collins, 2001.

Casperson, Dana May, *Power Etiquette: What You Don't Know Can Kill Your Career*, New York: American Management Association International, 1999.

Flach, Andrew and RoseMarie Alfieri, et al., *Combat Fat! The Complete Plan for Permanent Weight Loss*, New York: Hatherleigh Press, 2003.

Flach, Frederic, *Resilience: Discovering a New Strength at Times of Stress*, New York: Hatherleigh Press, 2004.

Gladwell, Malcolm, *Blink: The Power of Thinking Without Thinking*, 9th ed. New York: Little, Brown & Co., 2005.

Meshel, Jeffrey, *One Phone Call Away: Secrets of a Master Networker.* New York: Penguin, 2005.

Money Back Guarantee Terms and Conditions

Purchaser of this book can receive a refund of their full purchase price (up to $25.00 US) if their gross income has not increased by 25% within 1 year. Purchaser will have to supply the original purchase receipt; original Proof of Purchase seal from the book cover; an original copy of the book *The SELF, Improved*; a completed Reader's Test from the book web site below, and submit along with their tax returns for 2009 and 2010 as filed with the IRS. Redemption period ends 12/31/2011. This offer cannot be combined with any other promotional offer. Limit 1 per household. Send documentation and book to: *The SELF, Improved* Money Back Guarantee, c/o New York College of Health Professions, 6801 Jericho Turnpike, Syosset, NY 11791.

The purchase price of this book may be eligible for reimbursement through your employer's continuing education fund or program. See the web site for complete details at www.TheSelfImproved.com.

The Science of Self-Improvement and Wellness

New York College of Health Professions, a not-for-profit institution chartered by the New York State Board of Regents and located in Syosset, Long Island, New York, has been a leader in Holistic Education and Care for over 25 years. The College, which has national institutional accreditation as well as programmatic accreditation, offers undergraduate and graduate level degree programs in Massage Therapy, Acupuncture and Oriental Medicine; Certificate programs in Holistic Nursing for RNs, the Science of Self-Improvement and Wellness and a variety of continuing education workshops for professionals and the public. Its on-site clinics are some of the largest in the Northeast and provide holistic treatments to the community while serving as clinical internships for student practitioners. New York College also maintains a 35-acre modern medical facility in Luo Yang, the People's Republic of China.

The College has grown remarkably in the past several years and will continue to develop new educational programs as well as expand into many new areas. *The SELF, Improved* was written as an accompanying text to the 24-credit interdisciplinary Science of Self-Improvement and Wellness Certificate program—a program designed to enhance the motivation and employment skills of people entering the workplace, as well as those currently employed. The program seeks to increase job satisfaction and, thereby productivity. It draws from concepts and methodologies in psychology, career counseling and sociology, in addition to holistic wellness and balance. The Science of Self-Improvement workshops are also conducted off-site at corporations and for the general public. Additional information about New York College of Health Professions can be found at www.nycollege.edu.

243

About the Author

Donald Spector is one of the world's most prolific inventors. His patents and products in consumer markets, healthcare technologies, telecommunications and Internet technologies have opened up billion dollar industries. He has worked with and licensed his products to many Fortune 500 and large corporations around the world including the Squibb Corporation which set up a separate division for his inventions.

Donald Spector has also been extensively involved in the sports and entertainment industries and was Chairman of Deco Discs, a record label that used his patented format for CDs, as well as having been a Broadway Executive Producer. He has been a Foreign Representative for the Board of Trade of Henan Province, the largest province in the People's Republic of China. Currently, Donald Spector is Chairman of New York College of Health Professions, Innovation Fund LLC and Catalyst Applied Technologies, Inc.

For nearly three decades he has advised some of the world's most powerful leaders.

Donald Spector lives with his wife Marion in New York City and Florida.

NOTES

NOTES

NOTES

NOTES